# A PHILOSOPHY OF EMPTINESS

D0813856

# A Philosophy of Emptiness

Gay Watson

REAKTION BOOKS

Published by Reaktion Books Ltd
33 Great Sutton Street
London EC1V ODX, UK

www.reaktionbooks.co.uk


First published 2014
Copyright © Gay Watson 2014

Printed and bound in Great Britain
by Bell & Bain, Glasgow

A catalogue record for this book is available from the British Library
ISBN 978 1 78023 285 0

# Contents

And the emptiness turns its face to us and whispers,
'I am not empty, I am open.'
Thomas Tranströmer, *Vermeer*

# Introduction

A true expression of emptiness might be a blank page, yet a philosophy of emptiness must travel further, explore deeper, engage with language. There is a visual and affective difference between our response to the space of the empty page opposite and to this block of text – a space in which to reflect or some*thing* with which to engage. Is your response to the space one of respite or irritation? To the text, relief or resistance? Do you embrace the emptiness or rush to fill it? Do you welcome silence or turn on the radio? Our response to emptiness is experiential and subjective. I think that one's initial and perhaps one's continuing natural reaction to emptiness may depend on whether one is a glass half-full or half-empty type of person. I hope to show that a philosophy of emptiness may provide ways to temper our initial or even dispositional tendencies. It may offer an alternative view to challenge the conventional supremacy of substance and the seen, leaving in its wake a greater attention to what is overlooked, the shadows and traces that are never absent from the empty page.

Between the experiential reality and our attempt to evade or to make sense of it, there is a gap, a distinction and space for choice. Another gap opens between the term 'emptiness', which in English, unattached to some substance that something is empty *of*, is unfamiliar, even uninviting, and a 'philosophy of emptiness', which I will attempt to show may resonate with interesting and helpful echoes from many fields of inquiry. I hope in the following pages to journey through these gaps, exploring the landscape as we travel.

Emptiness may be experienced as empty of absolutes, empty of permanence and empty of independence, yet *not* empty of existence and meaning. Emptiness as insubstantiality may provide an alternative to our philosophies of substance; a middle way between *is* and *is not*, and the stark choice between existence and nothingness. Empty space may be space for possibility and contemplation, just as silence may hold an opening for quiet and the potential for sound. On the other hand, emptiness may be experienced only as meaninglessness, as utterly devoid and totally nihilistic.

A quick trawl through dictionaries, compendia of quotations and thesauri demonstrates the privative understanding of emptiness in the English language. 'Void of contents, want of substance, inability to satisfy desire, vacuity, inanity' are but a few definitions of emptiness given by the *Shorter Oxford English Dictionary*; the *Oxford Dictionary of Quotations* provides empty hearts, empty glasses and the empty words of a dream; while *Roget's Thesaurus* points to bareness, void, vacuity, vacancy, hollowness, shell, no man's land, waste and desolation among its list of synonyms. As a word, emptiness denotes lack; as a feeling, it connotes anxiety. However, a deeper, more contemplative and more philosophic inquiry may allow us to move from raw feeling and conventional usage to a broader consideration that takes account of both lack and what is lacking, and perhaps what it is that encompasses both, which may lead to an understanding that without emptiness there can be no fullness. Privation or potential. Embrace or evasion. By exploring such ideas we may follow a trail that is both familiar and strange.

In the vast space of emptiness, I start here with the experience, and from there move on to consider the word and concept and its translation from East to West. I then reflect on practice, exploring philosophy in the earliest Greek use of the term as love of wisdom, with the intention of a path to the good life, and consider practices of attention that supported such philosophy. From this existential beginning I turn to the philosophies of emptiness, travelling back in time and eastwards in space, to Buddhism and Taoism, two ways of thought and practice that very early produced the most comprehensive understanding of emptiness and paths to engage with it. After this I stay in the past but turn again from the East towards the West to follow traces of emptiness, and in so doing uncover some little-considered byways in the history of ideas.

While echoes of Taoist and Buddhist concepts and practices of emptiness are to be heard early on in Hellenistic philosophy, they are relegated to the margins of a history predominantly dictated by Christian beliefs. It is more generally not until centuries later, towards the second half of the nineteenth century, that emptiness reappears as a considered trope in Western traditions. However, from this time onwards in all branches of culture we find a collapse of earlier authority and presence, which opens up into emptiness and loss, and also possibility.

The later chapters of the book consider the resonance of emptiness in modern and contemporary culture. Here we often find description rather than prescription, and the delineation of emptiness as loss, rather than the teaching of comprehensive ways to deal with that breakdown of transcendent certainty. Yet we also see here pointers to possible paths through the openness that is revealed.

In the contemporary Western world, emptiness is commonly considered, if at all, as a blank, a lack, an absence of some*thing*. When I mentioned to friends that I was writing about emptiness, their first reaction was either that this was a Buddhist matter or, more often, puzzlement. What could be written about emptiness? Surely this was self-cancelling? This seemed to be followed by an inability to remember 'emptiness'. The term was usually replaced by another, and I was frequently asked how my writing on 'nothing' or 'silence' was coming along. Both are related terms holding aspects of emptiness, but neither succeeds any better than emptiness in encompassing the full meaning, that intertwining of dualities, lack *and* fullness, something *and* nothing, sound *and* silence.

The experience of emptiness at its most naked and negative is a cause of anguish, and it is not difficult to believe that much of Western religious and philosophical thought has gone about the task of erecting structures to defend ourselves against that apparent lack; gods, grounds, beliefs, absolutes and ideal forms stand to block our view of contingency. For emptiness is a profound human experience: 'Why is there something rather than nothing?' It is the first existential question. All myths and religions have been a response to the way man finds himself already 'thrown' into the world, in Heidegger's term. Gods, grounds and 'truths' have been set up as barriers or defences against nothingness, meaninglessness and *horror vacui*. It is not until such defences have begun to be questioned that the trope of emptiness and the question of loss of faith and of living with contingency appear regularly in Western culture.

Philosophies of emptiness arise in times of change. They arise from the struggle to find new ways to live. Philosophic and religious ways of life have relied upon beliefs, and when those beliefs are challenged or vitiated through scientific knowledge and political or social change, there are three main choices of response. First, we can find another subject of belief, knowing now that this view may be as susceptible to change as the previous one. Second, in the face of all evidence to the contrary, we may choose faith over reason, holding on to our old belief in a fundamentalist fashion in defiance of all evidence. Or third, we may contemplate change and impermanence themselves rather than the beliefs that hold them at bay.

Philosophies of emptiness are those that come from the third choice. Very often, rather than appearing as fully fledged theories, the traces of emptiness first appear in art, literature and even science as we struggle to find a philosophy that can acknowledge emptiness and loss of authority without pitching into a blank nihilism.

The deification of the sun that returns each morning, of spirits underlying natural features, of a god in the shape of man – all these present attempts to explain life, to defend ourselves in different places and historic times against a life empty of meaning, a life without some kind of transcendental necessity or guarantor. Man is the only creature that is conscious of its inevitable death; that, aware of its finitude, is future-oriented and seeks meaning outside itself. Our inevitable physical death remains the most unspoken topic of our daily lives, yet is unavoidable and casts its shadow. It is this shadow and this understanding that we see expressed in the work of many modernist cultural figures, such as Rilke, Beckett and Heidegger, who no longer subscribed to the solace of religion and the philosophies that had traditionally been the preeminent methods of defence from the anguish that this causes. Moreover, while we may find that much philosophy or religion provides an escape or defence against the feeling of emptiness, a philosophy *of* emptiness will proceed through an embrace of contingency.

It may be that cultures which embrace a sense of non-duality without difficulty deal best with the concept of emptiness, as they can hold the mutuality of lack and what is lacking. Buddhism and Taoism are two early Eastern ways of thought that present a considered 'philosophy of emptiness' in which emptiness is seen in a significantly different manner. It is an interesting, if incidental and perhaps rather frivolous fact, that research into fuzzy logic, a logic of more or less, rather than on or off, maps neatly on to a map of the Buddhist world. Such research was funded late in the West, only after the value of its technological application in the world of white goods – washing machines, dryers and the like – had been demonstrated in the countries of the East.[1] According to Bart Kosko in his interesting and amusing exploration of the topic, multivalent, fuzzy thinking comes from the Buddha, and the Western bivalent viewpoint from Aristotle. Shades of grey versus black or white.

Both Taoism and Buddhism, in particular the one fully formed and explicitly argued philosophical exploration of emptiness found in Buddhist thought, present a philosophy that is not one of lack. The Japanese philosopher Masao Abe has pointed out that the West in general gives priority and superiority to being over non-being, while in Taoist and Buddhist thought the idea of nothingness is ultimate. Thus their philosophies of emptiness, though somewhat distinct from one another, arise from an encounter between positive and negative principles that have equal force, and are mutually negating and mutually confirming. This and the fact that in Eastern thought this understanding of negativity is considered not only as an ontological issue, but also as an existential and soteriological one, gives rise to a view, or more importantly a *way*, of emptiness that transcends every possible duality, including that of life and death, transcending and embracing both emptiness and fullness.

When emptiness is considered so fully, a path may be seen to open up through contingency; that embracing contingency goes beyond it into suchness, the acceptance of reality in all its richness and uncertainty, and leads to a way of living well in the face of chance. Emptiness may be filled with defence and diversion, or it may be explored, found serviceable and even played with, as discussed later. The distinction between embrace and evasion is so significant that deep consideration of this philosophy might make us question whether emptiness is the correct translation for the term commonly translated thus. It may also, perhaps more importantly, make us reconsider wider ideas of emptiness, the existential reality that is reflected in so many areas of contemporary culture.

An Internet search for 'philosophy of emptiness', produces thousands of entries. By far and away the majority refer, in one way or another, to Buddhism, a philosophy of emptiness I explore at length. Here I just want to consider the Sanskrit term *sunyata* (*shunyata*) that is usually translated as 'emptiness'. Its root is the Sanskrit *svi* or *sva*, which denotes hollowness and swelling, as of a seed as it expands. Thus Buddhist emptiness in its very etymology holds a hint of fullness that is lost in its English translation. In a contemporary commentary to one of the key texts of Mahayana Buddhism, the Heart Sutra, Mu Soeng points out that in Sanskrit language, *sunya*, empty, was also the word chosen for zero, a concept that came into being with the great Sanskrit grammarian Pāṇini around the fourth century BC. Zero, he says, is a round circle with nothing inside, denoting the 'essential contentlessness of the phenomena. In other words, manifestation without essence'.'

Even in English the usage of 'emptiness' as a noun is misleading. Emptiness is not a thing, nor even a state of being. It is perhaps a state of becoming, a process, part of a verb – of an emptying out or being empty of something – and like everything else is lost without a context, without the world of everyday reality, of the things that other things may be full or empty of. The manner in which we reify it and abstract it is an example of the very psychological tendency that the Buddhist philosophy of emptiness is designed to mend; that is, the manner in which we endlessly try to solidify and grasp on to our experience, to make of the slippery and ever-changing process of life something solid to which we can cling, which will give structure and meaning to contingency.

To translate the term as 'the Void', as has often been done, compounds the problem, making it into not only a noun but also a proper noun, a thing with transcendent and mystical properties, an absolute, another defence against chance. We can only save ourselves from these mistakes, say Buddhist texts, by acknowledging 'the emptiness of emptiness', the understanding that emptiness too is contingent, dependent and contextual. Once we make a dogmatic 'belief' of emptiness, we have set up another false god or illegitimate transcendent, just as many of today's atheist writers can only be described as evangelical in their atheism. The true path of emptiness almost sneakily attempts to evade any such attempts to pin it down to anything more than the ever-changing kaleidoscope that is reality.

There have over the years been other attempts at translating *sunyata* that might evade this misconception: 'openness', 'transparency', 'momentariness', 'transitoriness', 'nowness' and, perhaps most interestingly, 'relativity'.[3] However, it is 'emptiness' that has pervaded, so we need to look closely into its early usage to see what is intended by the term. The one early and profound philosophy of emptiness sees it as the other face of suchness, that is, reality as truly understood. Its teachings then present a way to comprehend how things really exist and how we may live more happily in conformity with such understanding. That something is empty of essential lasting identity allows it to be changeful, moving and dependent upon an ever-altering web of causes, conditions and linguistic designation. This seems both very different and far richer than mere lack.

Once you start to peer through the spectacles of emptiness, you can find its traces in the strangest and most familiar of places in our contemporary world, particularly in the sphere of the arts. The major British contemporary art competition the Turner Prize provides several examples. One year it was awarded to a work that comprised a light randomly going on and off in an empty room. Another year the prize went to a 'sound sculpture', an invisible non-object that filled and changed space and experience; no object, just the trace of a voice that was initially installed under three bridges in Glasgow. That same year another contender painted pictures of absence. Based on well-known and controversial news stories, the paintings, while formally conventional, lacked their main subjects, who were indicated only in the titles and backgrounds.

The world of pop music provides an even stranger example that contrasts nicely both the idea of emptiness as lack, with its concurrent desire for consumption, and emptiness as something different, something more interesting. In an attempt to thwart the commercial hijacking of the Christmas popular music charts in the UK by the promoters of a blockbuster TV talent show, alternative songs have been heavily promoted. One year the unlikely 'number' chosen for the rival candidate was John Cage's infamous $4'33''$. This was a work Cage first presented in 1952, in which a musician came on to the stage, sat down at a piano, closed the lid, then remained static and silent for the given time, merely opening and shutting the piano lid to distinguish the score's three movements. More than 50 years later a group of well-known musicians came together to reproduce the event and offer the subsequent 'work' for sale and digital download. Various suggestions have been put forward concerning the initial intention behind Cage's piece: perhaps it was a critical response to the filling of silence with distraction and muzak; a demonstration that there is never absolute silence, that silence is just the background to sound; or an invitation to listen and to attend to sound without discrimination. I think that there is some truth in all these suggestions, but most likely the last response is most accurate, as Cage said: 'wherever we are, what we hear is mostly noise. When we ignore it, it disturbs us. When we listen to it, we find it fascinating.' He additionally said that he wanted his work to be free of his own likes and dislikes, and that 'I have felt and hoped to have led other people to feel that the sounds of their environment constitute a music which is more interesting than the music which they would hear if they went into a concert hall.'[4] He also wished to show that there is no such thing as silence, and at the time was inspired by another example of artistic emptiness, Robert Rauschenberg's *White Painting* series of 1951, which Cage described as 'airports for particles and shadows. A way of making emptiness visible.'[5]

The success of the piece, and the reason for its notoriety and continued relevance, probably comes from the fact that it gives rise to all these interpretations and plays humorously with the concept of emptiness. In contradiction to King Lear's pronouncement that 'nothing will come of nothing', both the experience of the listener and subsequent inquiry and reflection arise out of the work. In fact in a recent book I read that Cage also said of $4'33''$ that 'it opens you up to any possibility only when nothing is taken as the basis. But most people don't understand that as far as I can tell . . . But the important thing . . . is that it leads out of the world of art into the whole of life.'[6] The other side of emptiness is reality as truly understood as the endless, ever-changing kaleidoscope of becoming – perhaps an interpretation that the writer of an essay in the Tate magazine overlooked in a piece entitled 'The Void', when asking how close to nothing an artwork or an exhibition can go.

Such paradoxes, the play of silence and sound, substance and space, emptiness and fullness will, I hope, weave in an illuminating manner through these pages. A philosophy of emptiness concerns a considered response to experiences of emptiness. There is the way of avoidance and the way of attention.

# ONE

# Experience

With the loss of ground, what remains is shared practice. Giving grounds (must) come to an end sometime. But the end is not in ungrounded presupposition: it is an ungrounded way of acting.

Ludwig Wittgenstein, *On Certainty*

Men have talked about the world without paying attention to the world or to their own minds, as if they were asleep or absent-minded.

Heraclitus, trans. G. Davenport

Since emptiness occurs initially as a feeling, an existential response, one of the main themes that runs through this exploration is that of experience. Discussion of emptiness must be, in the phrase of the anthropologist Clifford Geertz, 'experience-near', close to our felt experience. If, as suggested, much of Western religion and philosophy has been a defence against feelings of emptiness, we must look both at attempts at escape and distraction, and at attention and acceptance, at silence and sound, emptiness and form. A careful exploration of emptiness entails not only or even theory, but necessitates practice involving both mind and body; emotion, sensation and intellect. It is a path.

'Emptiness is the track on which the centred person moves.' So wrote the Tibetan philosopher Tsongkhapa at the end of the fourteenth century.[1] And what is our personal experience of emptiness? I fear that most of us are not centred persons and that our tracks are usually ones of privation rather than paths. Emptiness may not always be the name we give to it, but I am sure that we have all felt the anguish of sleeplessness at 3 a.m. when all the worries that beset us become monsters, and behind them lurks the biggest monster of all, the question 'what is it all for?' Living with change, with recognition of impermanence, with loss of all kinds, leads us to question the purpose of existence, to ask what is the meaning of our life. This experience in some form is one most of us have had at some time, and a philosophy of emptiness, understood both subjectively and in the light of others' experiences, may lead us out of loss and into that other side of difficult experiences to appreciate that it is this understanding that may make us more resilient.

However, many people's first reaction when I asked them what emptiness meant to them was that it was something that required filling. As one friend replied to this question: 'vacuum–vacant–nothing'. And that, I believe, is the general response of our culture today. Emptiness connotes something that is missing, something lost, and the space of emptiness, of uncertainty and silence, is a space that we must quickly fill – with distraction, action and a search for a new certainty.

The desire for certainty and permanence wrapped in substance is surely the deepest desire humans have, even when not acknowledged explicitly. The poet Edward Thomas described it most beautifully as 'the never more than lightly sleeping human desire of permanence'.[2] We may seek it in absolutes, in substance or on the path of attention rather than avoidance. Careful attention to the whole of experience and a holding back from the reactive filling up of uneasy space may lead us to the realization that what we feel we have lost, permanence and certainty, might be something we never possessed at all. Perhaps then we may see that what is truly lost is only the illusion – of permanence and presence – and that in losing this we have gained a better understanding and a resilience against future loss. 'The moment we recognize an illusion as illusion, it ceases to be illusion and becomes an expression or aspect of reality and experience.'[3]

In the thoughtful language of Japanese philosopher Nishitani Keiji, a language that may be less familiar than the experiential feeling, we have moved in two steps. The first is from ordinary being to nihilism, a questioning and letting go of absolutes, permanence and certainties that are reassuring but ultimately false. This nihilism he sees as a *relative nothing*. Nishitani suggests that if we can move on from there, we may in a second step arrive at understanding *absolute nothing*, which he describes as emptiness *sive* fullness, which reinstates being, but within a different understanding of potential and fullness in acceptance of impermanence and contingency. This move, from feeling to understanding, from privation to path, is achieved through familiarization and attention.

Explicit Buddhist teachings on emptiness and conditioned or dependent arising (which are explained in chapter Two) are grounded in the meditative experience of the Buddha, which revealed to him the way things really exist. In turn the teachings are to be realized by followers through practices of awareness and contemplation. The revelations of the early Hellenistic philosophers were also not mere theoretical wordplay, but meant as guiding principles to practices of awareness. *Philosophia*, the love of wisdom, had a noble aim: to enhance *eudaimonia*, the good life, the life of virtue that led to well-being and serenity.

Explorations of emptiness by contemporary artists and psychologists similarly arise from awareness and experience, though they are frequently descriptive rather than prescriptive. Yet by illuminating and bringing attention to the problems and the experiences, they may enhance our ability to deal with them. Without attention we can only react unthinkingly, according to habit. Considered choice and wise action can only arise from awareness.

It was interesting that when I posed the same open question as to the meaning of emptiness to two artist friends, they both responded with positive answers. 'Relaxation, letting the mind empty, a wonderful feeling', said one. 'Reaching a state when the mind is free from fault and worry, at which you are receptive to what is going on', said the other. This may be the distinction between the feeling of emptiness and a philosophy of emptiness, the transition being the process of attention, for in the exploration ahead it is in the work of artists of various kinds as much as philosophers that we will find expressions of emptiness that go far beyond mere lack.

Significantly, the term 'meditation' in the Tibetan language is frequently translated into two somewhat dissimilar English terms: 'familiarity' and 'cultivation'. Any 'experience-near' discussion of emptiness will have to take a detour through practices of attention. We find these in the fields of Buddhism and Taoism, in Hellenistic philosophy, and in the practices of contemporary Western artists, musicians and thinkers. Attention is a skill, a practice that may be cultivated and enhanced.

Meditation is not something mystical or spiritual, despite the whiff of exotic orientalism that somehow adheres to it. It is merely a practice of attention; a being present with a kind of meta-attention that pays more notice to the very process of attending than to its content. It is a cultivation of deliberate physical and mental stillness, evading the usual distractions, and of watching the way our minds work and seeing things more purely, enabling us to notice the distinction between the thing seen, the thought thought, and the feelings and mental chatter that quickly surround that first moment of attention. We should not expect some form of transcendental experience, but we should examine such expectations or wishes.

I fear that in the West many new meditators arrive at the practice in search of some life-changing or 'spiritual' experience. It could be more helpful for most people to regard meditation like they do cleaning their teeth, as 'mental' rather than 'dental' hygiene. Though I am often concerned about the presentation of 'mindfulness' entirely without any historical context as a purely mental or physical health event, I can see this is useful as an antidote for our anxious achievement-oriented search for a 'spiritual' experience, a kind of grasping, albeit spiritual, that certainly Buddhist practice is intended to release us from. As at the beginning and end of the day we clean our teeth, so we may cleanse our minds with a brief period of quiet and reflection, a moral rather than oral cleanliness.

There is no 'good' or 'bad' meditation, concerning content at least. The intention of meditation is to be present. If we are bored, we should examine our boredom. If we are distracted, we should notice our distraction without judgement. Gradually, through practice, we become more adept in separating out thinking, imagination, sensation and feeling from the sense of ownership, story and action that we habitually impose on them. Thus slowly we may become more attentive to what is around us. As the poet Gary Snyder says, 'Meditation is not just a rest or retreat from the turmoil of the stream or the impurity of the world. It is a way of being the stream.'[4] Formal practice on the cushion is practice for mindfulness in action in everyday life.

This is the clear and undistracted awareness of being present *now*. What will we find? We will certainly find frustration at the wildness of the mind, which may at times turn into amazement at its endless invention and ability to leap from here to far there in the space of a breath. We will surely find boredom, irritation, sadness and joy. In a detached and receptive manner we are asked to notice what is happening in the moment, then to let it go. Thus we separate what we feel, see and hear from our emotional and intellectual reactions. Doing so, we may develop a kind of acceptance or tolerance for our experience. If we notice our dislike of sitting still but refrain from jumping up and engaging in distracting behaviour and continue to sit, noticing the physical sensation and the mental revulsion, transformation may slowly occur. By sitting with and accepting whatever occurs with a kind of receptive yet non-judgemental curiosity, we may go through the pain or the boredom towards a different experience. At the very least we can gain an understanding of how quickly our emotional expectations and reactions attach themselves to our bare experience. Gradually we may find that we are able to live our daily lives with a little more time and space that opens up around each experienced moment as we bring to light a gap between feeling and action, between thought and thinker.

The two major sutras or teachings about meditation in the Buddhist canon, found in the Majjima Nikaya, the collection of the middle-length discourses of the Buddha, can hardly be bettered today in their exhortation to pay attention firstly to our breath, and in so doing to expand attention first to the body and physical sensation; second, to our feelings, whether initially pleasure, pain or indifference; third, to the mind; and fourth, to the contents of our mind, the mental objects that fill our attention. The initial focus on the breath brings body and mind together, then acts as an anchor or harbour to bring the wandering mind back to focus as it inevitably gets pulled away, seduced by sound, sense or thought, into its habitual, drifting paths.

Thus meditation can be both analytical and expansive, a practice that enlarges the ground of consciousness by helping us to remain open to experience, rather than filtering it through our predispositions of habit, usage and fear. As Snyder writes: 'Meditation is the problematic art of deliberately staying open as the myriad things experience themselves.'[5] He goes on to say that poetry is one of the ways in which the myriad things are enabled to 'experience themselves', and likens this to zazen, the meditation practice of Zen Buddhism. I am sure we all have a favourite poet or poem that illustrates this. I think of the poet Mary Oliver's suggestion that to sit quietly in a lovely, wild place and listen to the silence is also a poem.[6]

Acts of meditation quickly teach us experientially that there is no one in charge; there is no governor self that rules the mind. And there are no thoughts or feelings that are permanent. Meditation provides rich, experiential lessons in impermanence, non-selfhood and emptiness, as well as the richness of what is left when these are acknowledged and lived with. If we can take the time and space to watch the way our minds work, rather than always concentrating on the content of our thoughts, we may gradually gain greater control and self-knowledge. Watching the mind, we may notice when the narrative of 'I' and 'mine' co-opts each fresh perception and twists into our default emotional tracks; then, through clearing the mind from its endless preoccupation with self, we may replace unthinking reaction with choice.

Nor is this just a Buddhist or Eastern concern. One of the most fascinating books on philosophy, taking a path often ignored, is that of Pierre Hadot, who addresses the theme of philosophy as a way of life. Based on his studies of Greek and Roman philosophers, Hadot became concerned with presenting and interpreting this philosophy not as a theoretical construct, but as a method for training people to live and to look at the world in a new way, as the authors originally intended. The intention of such philosophy, according to Hadot, was therapeutic – to cure mankind's anguish; and transformational – bringing inner freedom. Above all it is concerned with a way of life. To this end Hadot distinguishes between philosophical discourse, the discourse of the academy, and philosophy itself, a spiritual exercise that effects the transformation of the individual's life. I shall return to Hadot later, but here I would just like to emphasize his illumination regarding philosophy as an embodied way of life, concerned with practices whose intention is therapeutic and transformational; to heal our misapprehensions and alter them to concur better with reality so that we may acquire wisdom and freedom. Wisdom is not merely concerned with knowledge, but also enables us to 'be' in a different way, a way that may be free of anguish.

Hadot considers that the loss of the idea of philosophy as a way of life began with Christianity. In the beginning Christianity was presented as a philosophy and a path, but gradually a distinction grew between theology based on faith, and reason. Spiritual exercises were divorced from philosophy and integrated into Christian monastic practices, while philosophy itself became a theoretical, abstract and disembodied activity of reason. The scholastic university was, according to Hadot, the initiation of philosophic discourse, beginning the divorce of philosophy from an embodied search for the good life. Hadot does state, however, that 'this is not to say that modern philosophy has not rediscovered, by different paths, some of the existential aspects of ancient philosophy'.[7] We shall return to this later.

Hadot writes of philosophizing in Stoicism and Epicurianism as a continuous act, which had to be renewed moment by moment. He defines that act as an 'orientation of the attention'. He specifically mentions exercises of meditation on dogmas, on the finitude of life, examinations of conscience and an exhortation to live in the present. This, most interestingly, demonstrates that meditation in both the East and West shared a common focus. 'Attention to the present moment is, in a sense, the key to spiritual exercise.'[8] The tradition, however, continued over the centuries to flourish more strongly in the East.

The contemporary French philosopher Roger-Pol Droit published a strange and lovely little book in 2001, the English translation of which is titled *Astonish Yourself! 101 Experiments in the Philosophy of Everyday Life*. It calls itself an 'entertainment' and is a manual of 'everyday adventures' intended to enable the astonishment that the author considers gives rise to philosophy. These are all exercises of attention: 'the idea is to provide tiny moment of awareness' induced by exercises that range from the small – 'walk in the dark'; 'shower with your eyes shut'; 'follow the movement of ants' – to the vast – 'imagine your imminent death'. All offer imaginative ways to orient one's attention, to bring awareness to the contingency and the wonder that we daily fail to acknowledge.

Aspects of the meditative mind occur in many fields. In psychoanalysis Freud encouraged his trainees to cultivate a very similar state of mind that he called 'evenly suspended attention'. He suggested that there should be no note taking, and that everything should be received with equal and non-judgemental attention, a necessary counterpart on the part of the analyst to the requirement that the analysand should communicate everything that comes to mind, holding nothing back in the play of free association.

The same kind of attention also occurs in the arts, both in the artist's process of creation and also in a work's reception. Snyder has suggested that

> What meditation does for an artist or a craftsperson is
> to keep them open to seeing and hearing and feeling an
> Emptiness that is full of everything so it can respond to
> everything, everything can be in it.[9]

The artist Marina Abramović has written about of the experience of creating her series of performance works, *Nightsea Crossing*, which involved sitting silently for hours at a time in museum spaces. She describes how 'Nothing was happening on the physical level, but everything was happening on the mental level', and continues:

I started to attain high levels of meditation . . . which I could not explain and only later learned can be achieved with the Buddhist tactics . . . My entire relation to Buddhism came out of doing performances, through pure experience . . . first experience then the knowledge. Normally it's the other way around.[10]

The attention that artists bring to their creation invites the same response from the viewer, particularly today when so many artists ask for participation, not mere passive reception. Some art, and particularly much of the contemporary work I consider later, reflects and demands mindful awareness and a careful quality of attention.

Contemporary neuroscience also demonstrates the value of practices of attention, showing that they have physical results within the brain structure that alter subsequent experience. We know now about neuroplasticity, the process by which experience actually sculpts the brain. Experience alters the way our brains work and even their structure. Brains can be 'rewired', influencing the patterns of neuronal firing, forging new connections and even promoting the formation of new neurons. Neurons that commonly fire together, wire together, in the words applied to the work of the pioneer psychologist Donald Hebb. For example, the brains of violinists show significant strengthening in the areas concerned with the fingers of the left hand, used for fingering. Because of this neural reflexivity, we see that development is a two-way process. Our genetic inheritance affects our experience, and in turn our experience may become instantiated in our brains. Though development is strongest in the early years, we now know that neuroplasticity continues throughout our life. Moreover, this process is significantly strengthened when the activation of specific neural circuits occurs in conjunction with the activation of processes of attention. Perhaps this proof that we are literally creatures of habit may encourage us to choose our habits wisely. We can acquire skills that can change our brains and our experience. Recent experiments have shown significantly greater development in parts of the neocortex concerned with feelings of well-being and compassion in the brains of long-time meditators than control groups of both non- and short-term meditators. Such research is at an early stage, but its implications for well-being and the health of the mind are encouraging. Richard Davidson, the pioneer of emotional and contemplative neuroscience, points to practices of mindful meditation for the development of several different traits that may enhance well-being in *The Emotional Life of Your Brain*, which also describes his more than twenty years at the forefront of this scientific exploration.[11]

Neurology researcher James Austin has written about two distinct networks within the brain that employ distinct brain processes: a top-down, self-referential network that relates experience back to the self as experiencer, and a bottom-up, other-centred or allocentric network, more concerned with bare awareness. The self-referential mode is focused on and oriented towards the ability to act, while the allocentric network is more dependent on vision and hearing, answering the question 'What is it?' rather than the 'Where is it?' and 'How should I act?' of the egocentric process. These processes are complementary, and in the brain's passive resting state there is a spontaneous, intrinsic fluctuation between the activation of these networks, while in active experience the egoic or self-referential normally dominates. However, the latter is deactivated during attentional, goal-directed responses and when a sensory stimulus captivates attention. Austin suggests that deep-meditation practice may strengthen both these (bottom-up and top-down) processes of attention as they relate to the two main kinds of practice, concentration and insight, which may in turn strengthen the allocentric networks and loosen the hold of the egoic network.

Such times of insight, called *kenshō* in Zen Buddhism, enable awakening to realization of emptiness and suchness. As he describes, 'its realizations include emptiness (*sunyata*), and the comprehension of immanent Reality. This moment of Oneness confers the impression that all things are interrelated perfectly and eternally (*suchness*).'[12]

The philosopher Thomas Metzinger makes a different, but somewhat similar, suggestion: that while synchrony of neural responses plays a decisive role in figure–ground representation, deep meditation might reverse this process, turning background into figure. Such research is at an early stage. The important point is to appreciate that the phenomenological distinction between these contradictory ways of seeing and experiencing is instantiated in distinct neural networks, and to use that distinction to strengthen the neural substrates of the desirable pathways through cultivation. We look again at Metzinger's ideas and those of the psychiatrist Iain McGilchrist in a later chapter. In all these cases, the suggestion is that if we can become aware of the previously unconscious processes and biases of our minds, we may open space for choice in place of unconsidered reaction.

This may appear to have taken us some way from the discussion about emptiness. Yet throughout the exploration to come we frequently discover this alignment of philosophy, art and psychology when we are following the tracks of emptiness. Its meeting place is in the practices of attention – in contemplation, psychotherapy and artistic practice – where we find the willingness and the ability to go into our experience fully, to face up to life without absolutes, analyse our living experience and explore emptiness. What we find may be far from what, in fear and ignorance, we shun as being 'empty'. Attention to emptiness may leave us not with nothing, but with an appreciation of the intricate, ultimately ineffable construction that is our reality.

# TWO

# The Buddhist Philosophy
# of *Sunyata*

The core insight of the Buddhist tradition – the relentless
emptiness of phenomena – has profound implications for all
of us who are trying to understand the nature of life.

Andrew Olendzki, *Unlimiting Mind*

Buddhist thought is the home of the most developed philosophy of emptiness. The primary point to make is that this
philosophy of emptiness is also a philosophy of existence, not
of lack. It states that emptiness is inseparable from phenomena.
Emptiness, of essence, *is* the interdependence of all phenomena;
to be empty is to be dependently originated. Yet before we
begin to discuss this in detail, we must understand that while
there is a core of shared understanding, the many branches of
Buddhism do not teach an identical message. It is as much a
simplification and generalization to speak of 'Buddhism' as it
is to speak of 'Christianity'.

Early Buddhism represents the teachings of the historic
Buddha of our era; they were then transformed over time into
what we now term the Mahayana, or Greater Vehicle. Within
the Mahayana itself, major distinctions in the understanding
of emptiness occur between the Madhyamika and Yogacara
schools. The teachings of these distinctive schools of Indian
Buddhism then travelled northwards to what is now Tibet,
where they took on a noticeable flavour from Tantric practices,
and eastwards, where they mingled with ideas from Taoism and

Shintoism to form what we now consider as East Asian Buddhism. Most of the teachings of these different schools are now available in the contemporary West.

The term emptiness itself is rarely to be found in Early Buddhism, where the emphasis is on *anatta*, or not-self. Emptiness itself, *sunyata*, comes into play in the later Mahayana Buddhism, where the wisdom of emptiness becomes the centrepiece of Buddhist philosophy alongside *karuna*, or compassion, which is skilful action in the light of this understanding. Even within Mahayana teachings there are at least two major distinctions in the presentation of emptiness that are of importance in considering the topic.

I want to recognize the complexity of the picture while not getting bogged down in details that are not hugely relevant here, so I shall attempt to confine my discussion of emptiness within Buddhist thought by first considering Early Buddhism, second, the Mahayana – with particular emphasis on the Prajnaparamita teachings and the writings of Nāgārjuna – and third, a different understanding of the concept associated with Vajrayana and Yogacara teachings.[1]

## EARLY BUDDHISM

The Buddha Sakyamuni lived in the fifth century BC, a historical personage belonging to a clan living in what is now Nepal near the border with India. He was the son of the ruler of a minor principality at a time when cities were growing and there was much political and social change and unrest in the region. The myth-like histories of his life that are all we know about him tell us that his father kept him away from the normal experiences of daily life after receiving a prophesy about his son's future. The tales describe how with his charioteer the young prince made four trips away from his privileged life in the palace. On these trips he encountered for the first time an old man, a sick man, a corpse and a wandering monk. Seeing the serenity on the monk's face, the young man decided to leave his home and family in search of such composure in the face of suffering. After many years of austerity and failure to gain enlightenment even with the greatest teachers of the age, one day he took some ordinary nourishment for the first time after years of asceticism, and in deep meditation reached the enlightenment that provided the base for his subsequent teachings. In his first public teaching after this, he spoke what have become known as the Four Noble Truths: the truth that life is suffering, the truth of the cause of suffering, the truth of liberation from suffering and the truth concerning the eightfold path to achieve this. So it is usually presented. However, the truths are given not so much as facts, but rather as calls to action; suffering is *to be known*, the cause of suffering is *to be abandoned*, liberation from suffering is *to be realized*, and the path is *to be cultivated*.

The first truth asks us to know clearly that life itself from our ordinary standpoint is not, and can never be, entirely satisfactory or without suffering. We are drawn to crave what we like, which causes suffering when it is unattainable or disappears due to inevitable change and decay. We attempt to evade what we dislike, which causes suffering when we are unsuccessful. Perhaps the ultimate and inescapable unsatisfactoriness or suffering from the perspective of the egocentric individual is the fact of our inevitable death.

The second truth fundamentally relates to causation. Richard Gombrich, an authority on Early Buddhism, has pointed out that the great innovation of the Buddha was to reinterpret the pan-Indian doctrine of action, or *kamma* (Pali), *karma* (Sanskrit), in terms of intention, thus placing ethics, and I would add psychology, at the heart of Buddhist teachings or dhamma (*dharma* in Sanskrit), which become centrally concerned with analysis of how the mind works, and how willing comes about. As the Dhammapada, one of the earliest Buddhist texts, states:

We are what we think
All that we are arises with our thoughts.
With our thoughts we make the world.
Speak or act with an impure mind
And trouble will follow you
As the wheel follows the ox that draws the cart.[2]

The way of the Buddha is the way to understand and train the mind, presenting perhaps what we might call the 'first psychology'. Teachings demonstrate how ignorance of the way things really occur, and subsequent craving, are the causes of suffering.

The third truth relates to the possibility of liberation from suffering, and the fourth to the path that leads to this. The eightfold path is traditionally divided into three divisions – ethics, wisdom and mind training – and sets out the path of right understanding, right thought, right speech, action, livelihood, mindfulness, concentration and wisdom. The first step is that of right understanding, which refers to the understanding that all phenomena are impermanent, without inherent self and unsatisfactory, or the cause of suffering, if inappropriately understood. It is helpful to see the term *anatta*, or without self, in the context of the contemporary Indian belief in *atman*, the individual soul that is a spark of Brahman, the ultimate reality. The Buddha's new understanding of self and reality presented it as without this essence, without permanence, constructed and compounded, yet not as non-existent.

The way the self and all phenomena come into existence is termed *paticca samutppada*, or dependent origination. Everything that exists does so in dependence upon a network of causes and conditions. Underlying all the teachings is this central doctrine of dependent origination. Emphasizing its importance to his teachings, the Buddha said: 'One who sees dependent origination sees the Dhamma; one who sees the Dhamma sees dependent origination.'[3] More recently, this teaching of dependent origination has been referred to by the present Dalai Lama as 'the general philosophy of all Buddhist systems'.[4] The most basic presentation of dependent origination goes:

When this exists, that comes to be;
With the arising of this, that arises.
When this does not exist, that does not come to be;
With the cessation of this, that ceases.[5]

In its longer form, dependent origination in terms of the individual life is presented in links which are often referred to as the Wheel of Becoming, relating to cyclic existence. The most detailed, though probably neither the earliest nor the most fundamental, states:

When this exists, that comes to be; with the arising of this, that arises. That is, with *ignorance* as condition, *formations* [come to be]; with formations as condition, *consciousness*; with consciousness as condition, *mentality-materiality*; with mentality-materiality as condition, the *sixfold base*; with the sixfold base as condition, *contact*; with contact as condition, *feeling*; with feeling as condition, *craving*; with craving as condition, *clinging*; with clinging as condition, *being*; with being as condition; *birth*; with birth as condition; *ageing and death,* sorrow, lamentation, pain, grief and despair come to be. Such is the origin of this whole mass of suffering.[6]

Seen from the point of view of cessation, this cycle also points to the way of liberation, with the cessation of ignorance, the formations of mental dispositions and inclinations etched into our brains by habit will cease – and so on. Psychologically the key links are the first cognitive link of ignorance and the emotional link of craving. If we can acknowledge how things really are – that all things are impermanent and contextual, and without an in-dependent essence – we may be free from the endless struggle of desire and fear. If our selves above all are impermanent and changeable, why should we need to defend them so strongly, grasping to us all that we think will enhance them, and reacting with aversion to anything we believe may harm them? Freed from this misperception about self, we may live more happily – freed from the pride, hatred and grasping that arise from this ignorance, and thus liberated from suffering.

Another model of the person is that of *nama rupa*, called here mentality-materiality, more often translated both erroneously as mind and body, and as name and form. The latter is a better translation as the intention is to describe the formation of our experience and our resultant identity. In the Pali canon *nama rupa* is given as being comprised of feeling, perception, mental formations or dispositions, contact and attention. Later on this came to be considered synonymous with the *skandhas*, or aggregates, another model, which consists of the five psychophysical aggregates of form, feelings, perception, dispositions and consciousness. However, in the earlier presentation, as in the list above, consciousness is separate.

In one teaching the Buddha described consciousness and *nama rupa* as being like a pair of sheaves resting upon one another, each dependent upon the other; without consciousness there is no identity, but equally without psychophysical existence there is no consciousness. This has significant implications when seen in the context of the idealism of earlier Indian thought, and indeed of some later Buddhist thought.

These lists of components are often considered somewhat off-putting to those first interested in Buddhism. The important point to remember is their intention, which is to overcome the idea of the person as a single essential individual, yet to represent the experience and identity of the individual both subjectively and objectively.[7] These and other models of mind and mental states are all models of process rather than substance. For example, the sixfold base referred to above is that of the five senses, to which Buddhist thought adds a sixth or mental sense. All such models set out to disturb our normal sense of self, presenting not an achieved subject, but rather a *process of selfing*, the *creation of self*, which is always changing. It is not that a self does not exist, but rather that it does not exist in the manner we consider it to – as permanent, partless, independent and essential. From the Buddhist perspective ignorance arises when this process of selfing is grasped and identified with as an isolated individual entity, not as a changing process. The self, then, which in Buddhism is to be negated, is an illusion; it is the imposition of an identity with attributes of independence and permanence upon the foundation of the transactional or processual self that arises from the interaction of a network of causes and conditions.

This identification and reification of the process of selfing works, according to Buddhist thought, in three main ways, both emotionally and intellectually: through craving expressed in the linguistic form 'this is mine'; through conceit, demonstrated in 'this I am'; and cognitively, through holding false views of self, manifesting in the linguistic form 'this is myself'. Through these ways of self-creation and self-reinforcement, one identifies with a permanent, partless self-concept or self-image.

First there is the cognitive ignorance that misperceives the way self exists, that sees it as permanent, independent and essential, and on to this first misperception are added the emotional faults of desire and hatred, which seek to attach to whatever we like and feel will defend and bolster this self, and push away what we dislike and fear may harm it. Pride and craving adhering to cognitive misperception become the pivot around which an egocentric world arises.

It is not difficult to see how so many of our negative emotions, our fear and dislike, are directed at those who we feel are impinging on or disrespecting our 'self'; or how we feel that this same self will be enhanced by our latest purchase or even our latest haircut. In this way our experience of the world is always coloured by the needs of 'I', 'me' and 'mine'. The imposition of self as noun upon process self as verb is an aspect of our fear of contingency, and the subsequent grasping for a permanence and certainty that can never be achieved.

In one of the suttas, the Mulapariyaya Sutta, the Buddha goes through the manner in which the ordinary man views the elements of fire, water, earth and air, and the stages of meditation. Having contemplated each element the ignorant impose themselves on to each one, then consider them 'mine'. In contrast, awakened beings see each element directly, free from the need to impose themselves or their sense of possession on to them. This, says the Buddha, is due to the destruction of desire, hatred and delusion.[8] Such destruction of desire, hatred and delusion is liberation.

There are two sutras in the Pali cannon that, unusually for the Early Buddhist texts, use the word emptiness in their titles – the Shorter and Longer Discourses on Emptiness, but the term is used in a somewhat distinct manner from the way it is used later in the Mahayana. Here it is specifically related to meditation; emptiness is seen not as a philosophical idea but as an undisturbed physical space in which attention can be nurtured. Within such formal states, the monk is said to regard each stage 'as void of what is not there', but as to what remains there, he understands that which is present, thus 'this is present'. This is said to be 'genuine, undistorted, pure descent into voidness'.[9] In fact, such an admonition can usefully be kept in mind whenever we consider a philosophy of emptiness: to see what is not there and also what remains.

In another sutra in which the actual word 'empty' is used, one of the Buddha's disciples, Ananda, asks the Buddha: 'Venerable

38

sir, it is said, "Empty is the world, empty is the world." In what way is it said "empty is the world"?' He receives this reply: 'It is, Ananda, because it is empty of self and of what belongs to self that it is said, "Empty is the world."'[10]

The ethical and attentional tasks of the path are there to erase that solid sense of self that warps our every perception by imposing 'I, me, mine' on to bare awareness. Practices of mindfulness and meditation are taught in order to bring our attention to the ultimate unfindability of the self as we ignorantly consider it. Questions are suggested as to whether the self is the body, the feelings or the mind, all or none, to demonstrate the lack of essence and inherent existence of any such thing as the self. Other models are considered, for example the manner in which a sensory event occurs through the interconnection of causes and conditions, for example a sensory organ such as an ear, the object, a sound, a moment of ear consciousness and contact. Through deconstructing the solid sense of self by exposing its dependence on a network of factors, it is revealed to be impermanent, dependent on that which is other, or non-self; if this is not truly understood it is the cause of suffering.

Contemporary neuroscience is reinforcing this conception of the self as empty of essential existence, and demonstrating that it is a process, or construction of different processes. However, we still commonly believe and behave as if the self is a single identity, a thing rather than a process of creation. Psychotherapy illustrates the suffering that occurs when we identify with one aspect of this process of 'selfing'. Commonly we take on an identity that we inherit from our family or early experience (as the 'good girl', the 'naughty boy' or the 'little helper') and, getting stuck in this unidimensional identity, suffer when changed experiences and environments require different responses from us. If we know our selves as empty of fixed essence, as constructions and narratives, we may react more resiliently and flexibly to ever-changing circumstances, seeing in such lack of essence potential rather than privation. The daily acting self does exist, but not as an independent essence isolated from the processes that form it. The 'self' of which we speak would probably today be called an emergent process, one that emerges from the interaction and interdependence of other processes, such as physical form, feelings, and so on. The whole is both greater than its parts and inseparable from them. These models of process and emptiness were applied in Early Buddhism to selves, and then, as we shall see, extended to all phenomena.

## THE MAHAYANA

After the death of the Buddha, his followers divided into many different schools following different interpretations of the teachings. Traditionally the number of schools is given as eighteen, but it is unknown if this is an actual or mythical number, as far fewer have left specific teachings or traces that have come down to us today. However, over time a major shift occurred from the early schools, pejoratively known as Hinayana or the Lesser Vehicle (and for this reason now termed Early Buddhism), to the Mahayana or Greater Vehicle.

The Pali canon relating to the Theravada school, with its three divisions of rules for the monks called the Vinaya; the Suttas, or stories of the Buddha's teachings; and the later Abhidamma, or systematized teachings, is considered as representing the root texts of Early Buddhism. The major distinctions in the teachings associated with the Mahayana are a change in consideration of the Buddha from an individual teacher to a more cosmic understanding, a greater opening of the teachings to laypeople, and a shift from the individual path of the arhat, one who sought enlightenment for his own sake, to the path of the bodhisattva, who vows to set his own enlightenment aside until all sentient beings achieve liberation. This also reflects a concern in the Mahayana with the concept of compassion, which along with the wisdom of emptiness is one of the two pillars of Mahayana teachings. The other significant change was that the teaching of *anatta*, the emptiness of self, was expanded to that of *sunyata*, the emptiness of all phenomena, and even the emptiness of emptiness itself.

The locus of this teaching is found in the Prajnaparamita literature, a collection of texts of varying lengths dating from around the first century AD to several centuries later, which expound the teachings of the supreme wisdom of emptiness. Beyond these sutras that are considered to be the teachings of the Buddha, the central figure here is Nagarjuna, a philosopher and practitioner from southern India thought to have lived around the second century AD. The writings of Nagarjuna, along with later commentaries by other writers, formed the basis of what later became the Madhyamaka school, the school of the Middle Way. If the initial middle way taught by the Buddha in his first sermon was that of a path between asceticism and desire, the middle way now emphasized that between eternalism and nihilism.

Emptiness is taught as being grounded in, and indeed as being no other than, the very interdependence expressed by dependent origination (translated in the extract below as relational origination), that is, the emptiness of inherent existence or any self-sufficient essence in mutually dependent processes. In the dedicatory verses to the primary text of Madhyamaka Buddhist thought, the *Mulamadhyamakakarika,* Nagarjuna stated:

> I pay homage to the Fully Awakened One
> the supreme Teacher who has taught
> the doctrine of relational origination,
> the blissful cessation of all phenomenal thought
>     constructions.[11]

The specific method of Nagarjuna's argument is that of the tetralemma, a fourfold logic of complementarity rather than contradiction. He explains that due to dependent origination every event is marked by eight negations:

> Non-origination, non-extinction,
> non-destruction, non-permanence,
> non-identity, non-differentiation,
> non-coming (into being), non-going (out of being).[12]

Due to these qualities Nagarjuna sets out to prove the emptiness of all phenomena by a series of arguments that deconstruct every possible position held by an opponent by reducing it to absurdity. This method is applied to different topics: to time, self, anguish, seeing, walking and so on.

Towards the end of the work Nagarjuna declares that dependent origination (here translated as contingency) and emptiness are one and the same, and constitute the middle way of Buddhism.

> Contingency is emptiness
> Which, contingently configured,
> Is the middle way.
> Everything is contingent;
> Everything is empty.[13]

The well-known Vietnamese Buddhist teacher Thich Nhat Hanh presents a most poetic and easily understandable description of emptiness in relation to the page you are now reading:

> If you are a poet, you will see clearly that there is a cloud floating in the sheet of paper. Without a cloud, there will be no rain; without rain, the trees cannot grow;

and without trees, we cannot make paper. The cloud is essential for the paper to exist.[14]

Thus within the sheet of paper he includes clouds, rain, sunshine, trees, the logger, his food, his parents and finally you, the reader. All of these, in his term, 'inter-are' through their dependent origination. Emptiness is just the description of this interbeing from another perspective: that of the lack in each part of the process of independence and autonomy. Seen thus, we may understand that emptiness is possibility; that without which nothing is possible. As Nagarjuna explained:

When emptiness is possible
Everything is possible;
Were emptiness impossible,
Nothing would be possible.[15]

When emptiness is realized in this way, what we understand is suchness, and then:

Life is no different from nirvana,
Nirvana no different than life.
Life's horizons are nirvana's:
The two are exactly the same.[16]

The way we naturally apprehend reality is the conventional truth of appearance, the absolute truth of which is emptiness. These two truths are, however, inseparable; emptiness is not something other than the emptiness of independent existence of any thing, thus emptiness itself is empty. The supreme fault is that of reifying emptiness itself.

Buddhas say emptiness
Is relinquishing opinions.

> Believers in emptiness
> Are incurable.[17]

The sole canonical text that Nagarjuna refers to is the Discourse to Kaccana, which is from the Pali canon rather than later Mahayana texts and is the Buddha's response to an enquiry as to what is the right view. To which the Buddha replies:

> This world, Kaccana, for the most part depends upon a duality – upon the notion of 'there is' and the notion of 'there is not'. But for one who sees with complete intelligence the arising of the world as it happens, there is no notion of 'there is not' in regard to the world. And for one who sees with complete intelligence the ceasing of the world as it happens, there is no notion of 'there is' in regard to the world . . . 'There is,' Kaccana, this is one dead-end. 'There is not,' this is another dead-end. Without veering towards either of these dead-ends, the Tathagata teaches the Dhamma by the middle.[18]

The important thing to understand clearly is what the middle is, what is to be negated and what remains; how we can walk the knife-edge between eternalism and nihilism. As Nagarjuna stated:

> The Buddha rejected
> Both 'it is' and 'it is not'
> In His Discourse to Kaccana.[19]

The heart of the Buddha's teaching, according to Nagarjuna, is the understanding of emptiness, and the heart of understanding emptiness is to know that to be empty is to be dependently originated. When dependent origination is understood, so are the four truths – of suffering, origin, liberation and the path. Stephen Batchelor has suggested that the four truths may be seen as four ways of articulating the practice of emptiness: fully knowing *dukkha* (suffering) includes recognizing its *anatta/sunna* (not-self/empty) nature; letting go of craving is like Nagarjuna's statement that 'emptiness is the letting go of opinions'; *nibbana* (liberation) is, following Nagarjuna, emptiness itself; and the eightfold path is an empty track along which the centred person moves.[20]

Phenomena, like selves, exist, but not in the manner we naively think they do. They exist in dependence on causes and conditions, on their own parts and on the designations we confer on them by language and usage. They are dependently originated and thus empty of inherent existence. Understanding this, we can see, as the best-known example of Prajnaparamita literature, the Heart Sutra, explains, 'form is emptiness, emptiness is form. Emptiness is no different from form, form no different from emptiness.' The sutra continues by stating that this applies also to the other four *skandha*s, or aggregates, that make up the person: feelings, perception, dispositions and consciousness; all are empty. All phenomena are empty as they are ultimately without defining or inherent characteristics; they are thus neither created nor destroyed; neither pure nor impure; and neither deficient nor complete. The sutra continues, asserting how, in the light of emptiness, all the pillars of Buddhist teaching – the four truths, the five aggregates, the twelve links of dependent origination, and so forth – lack inherent existence. It ends with a probably later added exhortation to recite the mantra of the perfection of wisdom: '[Om] *gate, gate, paragate, pārasamgate, bodhi svaha.*' Gary Snyder has given a translation of this as 'Go, go, go beyond, go beyond beyond, Bodhi svaha.'

The Madhyamaka exposition of emptiness does not fail to turn its own doctrines back on to itself in teaching the emptiness of emptiness. Emptiness is the relinquishing of opinions, not the exchange of one opinion for another. The concept of emptiness itself, just as any other concept or phenomenon, may easily be the object of ignorant understanding and emotional grasping. This is an important point that is often overlooked and one to keep in mind in terms of more recent atheist and postmodern doctrines. It is perhaps timely to mention here that the second pillar of Madhyamaka teaching alongside the wisdom of emptiness is *karuna,* compassion. When one truly understands emptiness and interbeing, compassion for all that one is not separate from will naturally arise. At the same time, consciously arousing compassion may lead us to a better understanding of emptiness.

### THE THIRD TURNING OF THE WHEEL

The Madhyamaka presentation of *sunyata* is largely a non-mystical, immanent presentation of reality, and the limits of language and knowledge. Later, others felt this to be too negative, too cerebral and rational, and too difficult and even potentially nihilistic for followers of the Buddha's path. Their concern was the efficacy of any teaching for following the path, loosening the rational and emotional fixations that tie us to samsara and suffering, while not leaving us without hope of liberation. Based on this fear of over-negativity and on experience gained in meditation, a different conception of emptiness came into the teachings.

There are arguments within Buddhist polemics that make medieval Christian disputes about the number of angels on the head of a pin seem simple; I would wish to acknowledge this complexity rather than ignoring it, but without going deep into the thickets of the territory of more interest to Buddhist scholars or practitioners. However, there is an important distinction in the presentation of emptiness between the purely non-implicative Madhyamaka, one that supports 'the emptiness of emptiness', and one that presents emptiness as having its own qualities, a presentation that perhaps places more emphasis upon *tathata*, suchness, than *sunyata*, emptiness.

The teachings of Early Buddhism became known as the First Turning of the Wheel of Dharma, and the teachings of Madhyamaka as the Second Turning. These were then followed by a Third. Different schools take different turnings to be the ultimate teaching. Madhyamaka teachings are considered by the Tibetan Gelug school, whose head is the Dalai Lama, as the ultimate teaching of the Buddha. Other schools take the Third Turning to be ultimate. Here we are not concerned with the details of the history of the schools that propounded these teachings; I will merely say that the teachings of the Third Turning are to be found within the traditions of Yogacara and Cittamatra schools, and within some of the schools of Vajrayana or the Tantric Buddhism of Tibet. They also tend to be more mystical and more influenced by practices of meditation than by the more textural and rational studies of the Madhymaka argument.

The main distinction in these teachings is that the Two Truths – the conventional or relative, and the ultimate truth of emptiness that were presented in Madhymaka doctrines – are replaced by three natures: the imaginary nature, which refers to our erroneous normal understanding; the dependent nature, the understanding of all things as dependently arising; and the perfect nature, the ultimate nature of emptiness. Central to this Third Turning of the Wheel is the distinction between self-emptiness – as presented by the Madhyamaka – and other emptiness. Emptiness here, the 'other emptiness' of the Third Turning, is empty of all else, but not empty of its own nature. Rather than the emptiness of self, or the emptiness of self and all phenomena, here the emptiness and non-duality is that of the relationship between consciousness and object, knower and known – what remains is the nature of original mind.

Within the literature of the Tibetan school of Dzogschen can be found the most poetic expression of these teachings: 'The nature of mind in its purity is, like a stainless crystal ball: its essence is emptiness, its nature is clarity, and its responsiveness is a continuum.'[21]

Such teachings centre on the nature of mind, and it is sometimes difficult here to distinguish between the referent of the terms emptiness, mind and Buddha Nature. Mind is naturally awakened and present at the heart of all experience. Unfortunately, its natural clarity and luminosity are veiled by our innate ignorance and emotional dispositions. Recognition of its pure nature requires that this be 'pointed out' through the instructions of a master. Such teachings allow that this ultimate mind has qualities; its essence is emptiness, its nature is knowing and clear, and its activity is unimpeded. From the perspective of the Madhyamaka view, this reintroduces the danger of positing 'something', dangerously close to the *atman* that Buddhism deconstructed. To its adherents it allows followers to evade the potential nihilism inherent in 'the emptiness of emptiness', and is based upon various authoritative scriptures and backed by meditative experience.

How you want to see emptiness may, I think, be much a matter of personality or disposition: whether you tend towards devotion or are devotionally challenged; whether you see a glass as half full or half empty. However, there is no doubt that the strongest disposition is that of yearning after and clinging to certainty, and this neediness is in Buddhist terms seen as the very centre and cause of our misguided misapprehension of reality, which can only inevitably lead to anguish. The doctrine of emptiness is a remedy to dispel such misunderstanding, not something else to be clung to; emptiness and existence are complementary, not antagonistic. One must understand that, as Jay

Garfield, an authority on Nagarjuna, has stated; 'to be empty is not to be non-existent, to exist is to be empty.'[22] As Nagarjuna himself pointed out, to cling to emptiness itself is the final error.

Misconstruing emptiness
injures you
like mishandling a snake
or miscasting a spell.[23]

# THREE

# Following the Tao

Yen Hui said, 'May I ask what is fasting of the mind?'

Confucius said, 'Your will must be one. Do not listen with your ears but with your mind. Do not listen with your mind but with your vital energy. Ears can only hear, mind can only think, but vital energy is empty, receptive to all things. Tao abides in emptiness. Emptiness is the fasting of the mind.'

Yen Hui said, 'Before I heard all this, I was certain that I was Hui. Now that I've heard it, I am no longer Hui. Can this be called emptiness?'

Confucius said, 'That is it . . .'.

Chuang Tsu, *Inner Chapters*

Possibly around the same time when the Buddha lived in India, in China the sage Lao Tzu wrote the Tao-te-Ching, the founding text of Taoism. Lao Tzu is perhaps an even shadowier and more mythic figure than the Buddha. It is argued that perhaps he was not a single person but, like Homer, a compilation of several voices. At the end of the first chapter of his exploration of the Silk Road, Colin Thubron relates a story of how Lao Tzu, leaving China sickened by the corruption of court life, was persuaded to stay one last night in the Pass to the West, a night in which he transmitted the teachings that comprise the Tao-te-Ching. He relates how in the morning 'he remounted his black buffalo and disappeared into the West', which, suggests Thubron, was 'a metaphor for death'.[1] There are even accounts in China suggesting that Lao Tzu travelled west to India, where he was the teacher of the Buddha. However, general belief today is that if he was one person, he lived later than this.

If emptiness in Buddhism is a philosophical term referring to the dependently originated nature of phenomena, in Taoism it refers more to the source of all, and to a psychological attitude and state of mind in which this can be realized, characterized by simplicity, non-willing, quietude and frugality.

The Tao-te-Ching concerns the Tao, an almost untranslatable term usually designated the 'way' – the way things are, and the way we should comport ourselves to them. The first great principle of Taoism is the principle of the relativity of all qualities. The French philosopher Marcel Conche states that the Tao is nothing other than the river of Heraclitus, ever flowing, ever changing, without beginning or end.[2] As with the unity of opposites of Heraclitus, the Tao is grounded in polarity, the complementarity – not contradiction – of pairs of opposites, the best known being that of yin and yang, which signify negative and positive, feminine and masculine, soft and hard, and most profoundly, that of non-being and being. Each pair is seen as arising together and implying and depending on one another.

> Difficult and easy complement each other.
> Long and short contrast each other;
> High and low rest upon each other;
> Voice and sound harmonize each other;
> Front and back follow one another.[3]

The ultimate source is both empty and indefinable, the 'nameless' that is the source of all: 'For though all creatures under heaven are the products of Being, Being itself is the product of Not-being.'[4]

Only the Tao that cannot be named moves between the source and the 10,000 named things:

. . . it cannot be seen – it is beyond form

. . . it cannot be heard – it is beyond sound.

. . . it cannot be held – it is intangible

. . . an unbroken thread beyond description.

It returns to nothingness.[5]

'The Tao is an empty vessel: it is used, but never filled.'[6] It is not the manifestation of some (ontological) 'nothingness' but the vehicle through which enough space and emptiness are created for effects to unfold.[7]

Everything in the universe originates in the same breath-energy, chi, which according to the processes of its constitutive factors of yin and yang leads to all manifestation. Chi condenses and coagulates under the yin influence and forms beings; becoming desaturated and distilled under the influence of yang, it lets in spirit, which allows all that exists to communicate across its dynamic emptiness. Thus form and emptiness are both part of a single reality, of chi, partaking of both a material and a spiritual dimension. As described by Arthur Waley, 'looked at from anywhere, the world is full of insecurities and contradictions; looked at from Nowhere, it is a changeless uniform whole.'[8]

The French sinologist François Jullien draws attention to a distinction between Chinese and Western thought so fundamental that it is difficult to translate; a distinction that underpins their approaches to philosophy, painting and writing. He suggests that Chinese thought is structured by a logic of 'respiration' rather than the logic of 'perception' that led to the 'ontotheological' choice taken by Greek thought. Such a logic does not separate presence from absence, a separation, he notes, that 'in its foundation leads back to that of being and nonbeing'.[9] The initial choice between 'I breathe' and 'I perceive' defines what constitutes reality. The Greek choice of perception led to the priority of a conception of reality as an object of knowledge. The

Chinese choice, based on an experiential knowledge of breathing in and breathing out, led to the principle of a regulating alternation of emptiness and fullness from which the process of the world flows. Such a mode of thought based on the rhythms of inspiration and expiration that through the transfer of air continually communicate with one another, rests in continuous process rather than taking a position between presence and absence. Just as it hovers between presence and absence, so it also escapes both subjectification and objectification. Jullien points out that from the very first words of the Tao-te-Ching, 'a roadblock stands in the way of the opposition between being and nonbeing, since any distinction between "there is" and "there is not" now refers only to different stages in the coming about of the process of things.'[10] Existence is a proceeding forth from emptiness, the undifferentiated source.

Most fascinatingly, Jullien suggests that while Western philosophy has always followed the way of clarity; that as according to Descartes 'the things we conceive very clearly and distinctly are all true', the Chinese have always chosen to think of the foundational as indifferentiated. One interesting and I think convincing point that, according to Jullien, follows from this is that once Western philosophy had chosen the clear and the distinct, literature, by way of compensation, could become the realm of ambiguity, whereas in China, poetry and painting were always directly linked to the conceptions of Chinese, notably Taoist, thought. He suggests that the importance of the Tao-te-Ching lies in the fact that it takes us back to a place before thought divided into ontology, and that it is so allusive and laconic because it comes from that indistinction which opens on to the undifferentiated. He suggests that a kind of spiritual resonance is internal to the breath-energy that is chi.

Jullien finds it notable that the notion of the Void was not taken up by Western philosophers except in the materialist tradition of Democritus and Epicurus, which was, he notes, 'a disgraced tradition for the most part, which denies any separate existence to the spiritual and conceives of the soul as corporeal'.[11] The Void for the Western tradition became an object of debate, assuming the status of a hypothesis (of its existence or nonexistence) on which the entire system will depend. In contrast, for the Chinese it is not a subject of debate since it is an experience, a resource that is prior to any question of knowledge, which is indeed brought about only through emptiness. It is neither an object nor a subject, but an 'operative factor'. As Jullien is at pains to point out, the 'void' that we are encouraged to recover

> is less inherent than immanent: it is not the mani-festation of some (ontological) 'nothingness' but the vehicle through which enough space and emptiness are created for effects to unfold. Life can escape whatever confines it and regain its freedom, allowing it to remain open to unfettered transformation. Based on deliberate deontologization (and de-theologization), this *release* from meaning (from dogma, belief, truth) results in a depressurization of existence, which ceases to be episodic or forced.[12]

To follow the Tao one should align one's own course to be in harmony with this, for the Tao is that which alone is absolutely existent and of its own nature. To be in harmony with empti-ness and potential, one must free oneself of the obstacles that fill one up; one must empty oneself, become unknowable like the Tao, free from any specification from which limitations arise. A term commonly used to describe the ideal manner of comportment with the Tao is *wu wei*, which may be translated as 'non-action', 'effortless action' or 'without struggle'. This refers not to a forced tranquility, but to a course of action undertaken without effort or purposeful intention of gain, a way of acting in which human actions become as spontaneous and mindless as those of the natural world. To achieve such spontaneity truly, however, requires that the human be in alignment with the natural. The breath-energy that is the Tao and the way we can best align ourselves with this energy applies undividedly to our physical, mental and spiritual continuum:

> If you want to become full
> let yourself be empty.
> To become full, be hollow.[13]

A century and a half later, an equally mysterious writer, again possibly not one individual, Chuang Tzu, in the second most important Taoist text, elaborated on these fundamental themes of the way things are and the way one should comport oneself to be in harmony with this. 'Emptiness, stillness, limpidity, silence, inaction are the root of the ten thousand things';[14] the way gathers in emptiness alone.

> In the Great Beginning, there was nonbeing; there was no being, no name . . . If the Nature is trained, you may return to Virtue, and Virtue at its highest peak is identical with the Beginning. Being identical you will be empty, being empty, you will be great.[15]

'Emptiness thus, is the fasting of the mind', the freeing of the mind from all obstacles to align with emptiness and potential.[16] 'Be Empty, that is all.'[17] But this is not a static or positioned emptiness; it is the ability to go with the flow, to be resilient, to be without position. 'Empty, they may be still; still, they may move,'[18] just like, as T. S. Eliot was to note centuries later, the way a Chinese jar moves eternally in its stillness.

The best-known and most-loved story of Chuang Tzu is doubtless that of his dream of a butterfly, awakening to wonder whether he was a man who dreamed he was a butterfly, or a butterfly who dreamed he was a man. For Chuang Tzu expresses imaginatively and poetically the paradox and mystery of reality and representation. In the words of Burton Watson, one of the finest of Chinese interpreters, the first two chapters of the *Chuang Tzu*:

> together constitute one of the fiercest and most dazzling assaults ever made not only upon man's conventional system of values, but upon his conventional concepts of time, space, reality, and causation as well.[19]

Watson explains how Chuang Tzu, like Nagarjuna, uses every device of rhetoric to expose the reader to the ultimate meaninglessness of conventional values, in order to free them from their hold. Paradox, non-sequitur, humour and what he calls 'pseudological debate' are used, like the tetralemma of Nagarjuna or the koan of Zen, to disturb the expectations of listeners and jolt them into a different way of understanding.

There is no doubt that Taoist teachings, being very much complementary to Buddhist teachings, had a strong influence on Far Eastern Buddhism, through Chinese thought, to the Japanese Kegon (Huayan) school, with its teaching of mutual interpenetration and interdependence following the principle of non-obstruction. It is to Huayan that we are indebted for the wonderful image of the net of Indra, that multidimensional net with jewels at each node, in which each jewel contains the reflections of all others ad infinitum, an image that is to be found frequently in contemporary writing in many fields, expressing ecological relationships and the way the cosmos is implicit in each member. We see the resonance of the Tao in the *dō*, or ways, of Japanese culture: the way of painting, the way of poetry, the way of the tea ceremony or of archery. It is that quality that today is often and popularly called Zen.

It is perhaps due to the fact that much of Taoist thought was taken up into Buddhist teaching, and the poetic and logical challenge of the writings themselves, that there is much less literature about Taoism today. When investigating emptiness from a Buddhist perspective, the difficulty is to do justice to the huge array of primary, secondary and subsequent texts that have proliferated around the topic. Philosophical and doctrinal treatises, poetic expressions and manuals for practitioners woven around the theme are endless. On Taoist thought there is considerably less literature available. Another factor for this may be that the history of Taoism encountered a swerve in teachings, and much of its later writings were concerned with what we might term alchemy and the way to encourage long life, if not immortality. However, the main reason, I believe, is one of quality rather than history. Emptiness in Taoist thought is little concerned with linguistic expression. As some translators have rendered the first verse of the Tao-te-Ching: the Tao that can be taoed is not the real Tao.

## THE INFLUENCE OF TAOIST THOUGHT IN ART

The influence of Taoist thought, however, on Chinese life, philosophy and the arts, especially in the ways of painting, writing and even physical exercise, has been great. In Chinese thought human culture is seen as an extension of nature rather than in opposition to it. Thus its art 'reminds' us of nature rather than 'representing' it. Japanese painting and poetry unfolded from the same roots.

> Where Western art embraces imitation of nature as something essentially other – assuming the alienation of man from nature, the Japanese artist, imbued with the teachings of Buddhism and native Japanese Shinto . . . begins by assuming man and his art as indistinguishable

from nature, and seeks to achieve not a copy of the natural world by artificial means (words and paint), but an experience of oneness with nature.[20]

Jullien, having compared the Greek logic of perception to the Chinese logic of respiration, suggests that the unobjectifiable quality present in Chinese art comes from its manner of form unfolding from the foundation of what he translates as 'the fount of immanence' in a play of alternation between emptiness and fullness. The taking and giving back of form to and from the undifferentiated fount is the very act of respiration. The aim is not so much to represent reality as to produce it in the energetic exchange that encompasses both emptiness and form. This results in a sense of presence through embracing contingency that has no need for external support. It is not a presence of totality, but rather the understanding that in embracing both the emptiness of all forms and of duality between subject and object, everything is yet present to itself.

Jullien suggests that the Tao-te-Ching takes us back to a time and place before thought branched off into ontology;

the word *tao*, which serves as a signpost at that juncture . . . constantly points toward a modality of the real that, remaining upstream from any actualization and opening onto the undifferentiated, is not yet in the grip of disjunction.[21]

In remaining upstream from the place of disjunction, the image keeps present the fount of emptiness and potential. In poetry a similar notion serves to evoke the emptiness between words and the allusive quality of poetic meaning. This is a place of which the Western philosophies of presence were not aware.

Thus Eastern art is not an art of representation: its aim is not so much to represent objects or essences, but to record a play of energies. True representation lies beyond form, 'in that allusivity to the invisible dimension that permeates the concrete particularity of the strokes'.[22] Nor is the painter or poet separate from the subject of the painting or poem, or expressing him or herself through the content. Rather, the landscape or the content expresses itself through the artist, both participating in the same breath-energy and what Jullien calls 'sense-emotionality' or 'intentionality' that runs through both painter and painting, poet and poem – as the Japanese poet Bashō exhorted us to learn of the pine tree from the pine tree, and of the bamboo from the bamboo. Such energy incorporates both form and spirit that can reach beyond form.

In another essay, *In Praise of Blandness*, Jullien explores a sensibility foreign to Western thought, but central to Chinese thought, to illustrate this approach that is common to all the arts. Blandness, as he describes it, is not a weakening cut off from its source but a refusal of discrimination, and a closeness to source or potential that is prior to all distinctions. It has much in common with emptiness, being an openness, an indistinction that hesitates to prefer one taste to another so that no one thing can overwhelm the attention. In music there is an appreciation of silence; in poetry, blandness allows by its lack of differentiation an increase of potential in which meaning encompasses both presence and absence. Like emptiness, blandness does not represent, it rather 'de-represents', pointing to 'the sense of the emptiness inherent in all things'.

An important point, and one to keep in mind when considering contemporary art practice, is that this blandness applies to both the practitioner and the spectator or listener. Bland (*dan* in Chinese) also signifies inner detachment. It requires a transformation of both artist and audience. Saying that the bland is related to the idea of centre, Jullien explicitly likens this notion of centrality to the middle way of Madhyamaka, where 'centrality's value is found in its relation to emptiness', in transcending the opposition between existence and nonexistence, affirmation and negation. It is towards this understanding, he says, that the Chinese notion of bland leads us.[23]

This is echoed by Lee Joon in an essay accompanying an exhibition in 2007 entitled 'The Void in Korean Art', in which he explains how nothingness coexists with being, and becomes the dynamic, functional aspect of being; 'void in E. Asian painting is the space that mediates between being and nothingness'.[24]

Thus the aim of East Asian art was traditionally thoroughly different from that of classical Western art. The painter or poet does not attempt to reproduce or compete with nature through artifice, by duplicating natural scenes through such means as using perspective to simulate three dimensions in two to show the world from the perspective of a perceiving subject, but strives rather to encompass and implicate consciousness in the great play of energies that it presents. What is important is not the things themselves, but the relationships in space and the energy that infuses everything. As Jullien describes it, painters 'paint vectors of vitality not visual objects'.[25] A Chinese scroll painting offers us a perspective of the whole – the unity of the 10,000 things. As in painting, so in writing: 'the nonobject of painting corresponds to the nonthematization of the poem.'[26] Grounded in the same immanence, partaking of the same breath-energy, the reach of the artist and the writer is enabled to reach beyond representation.

Paradoxically, it would seem that at this point in time China, the source of this kind of thought, is rushing headlong down the occidental road of technology, capital and consumption, while the considered thought and arts of the West are expressing Taoist traits, such as an anti-theological bent, a philosophy of nature and rejection of man's domination, and a resultant concern for ecology that are much in tune, as Conche points out, with '*l'esprit de notre époque*', the spirit of our age.[27]

# FOUR

# Moving Westwards

Everything flows, nothing remains.

Heraclitus

Empty is that philosopher's argument by which no human
suffering is therapeutically treated. For just as there is no use
in a medical art that does not cast out the sickness of bodies,
so too there is no use in philosophy, unless it casts out the
suffering of the soul.

Epicurus

At around the same time as the teachings of Buddhism and
Taoism in China and India, there arose in Greece what we in
the West consider our philosophic and ethical heritage, the
foundations of our culture. Until recently Western philosophy
has generally been discussed in isolation from the philosophy
of Asia. However, research into the diffusion of ideas East to
West, and West to East, has shown this to be a misapprehension. Moreover, research into branches of Greek philosophy
outside the main Platonic and Aristotelian lines that so deeply
influenced Western culture have shown remarkable similarities
to the teachings we have explored in relation to Buddhism.

Contact between Indians and Greeks, and some trade
between the eastern Mediterranean and India, is known to
have occurred from ancient times. During the Presocratic
Upanishadic period, meetings would have occurred at the

Persian court. Later, Alexander the Great entered India in early 326 BC and established his headquarters at Taxila near the mouth of the Khyber Pass, a site that was already a meeting place for travellers and traders from all over India and a seat of higher learning. Interestingly, Stephen Batchelor suggests that the Buddha may have studied at Taxila himself, and if he did not, it is known that others close to him during his life had done so.[1] Taxila, the major city of the Gandhara region, the northern area of the Indus Valley, became known later as a centre for both Buddhist thought and Greek learning. It was the home of the Gandharan style of sculpture and of the Kharosthi script, in which Early Buddhist sutra texts have only quite recently been discovered. It is also the region where the Abhidharma developed, the teachings and texts that comprise the systemization and extrapolation of Buddhist doctrines from the narrative of the sutras. It is from this region, too, that the transmission of Buddhist learning began, from India to northeastern Asia and along the silk routes into China. Much evidence of this Graeco-Buddhist milieu and of Indo-Greek communities has been found: rock edicts set up by Emperor Ashoka that were carved in good literary Greek; proof that major Buddhist rock-cut temples were endowed by Greeks; the existence of Corinthian capitals on pillars that show Buddhas in sitting meditation amid acanthus leaves; and a coin that shows a picture of the Buddha alongside Greek characters.

Further evidence of Indo-Greek fusion lies in the text known as the Milindapanha, or the Questions of King Milinda. This relates to Menander, a second-century BC Greek king of an Indo-Greek kingdom who was considered to have become an arhat, or enlightened one. It is in this area also that the Prajnaparamita literature, the texts of emptiness, originated.

The influence of Indian ideas from the Upanishads and the Vedas on early Greek thought, and the diffusion of Greek influence into India through trade and the aftermath of the expedition of Alexander the Great, demonstrate a fertile exchange of ideas and knowledge. It is not my intention here to relay the arguments as to which way the influence worked and when, but only to express the intriguing overlap of content. This returns us to a theme expressed in chapter One concerning philosophy as a way of life. The philosophies that resonate with teachings of emptiness, in distinction from philosophies of presence, are those most concerned with supporting a way of life; they are concerned with eudaemonia and with therapeutic intent and actual practice rather than with theory. It is in the philosophies of Heraclitus, Democritus and the later schools of Stoics, Epicureans and in particular the Pyrrhonian Sceptics that we find the echoes of emptiness and a concern with philosophy as therapeutic.

There will be several themes that play throughout the philosophies we will consider: a concern with naturalism, with the senses rather than reason, with experience, ethics and practice. The earliest guide is Heraclitus (c. 535–475 BC). All that we know of Heraclitus comes from some often paradoxical fragments of text, and the reports of others. Heraclitus is probably best known for his statement that 'all is flux' or process. He believed that in a realm of flux or becoming, nothing could be said to exist in and of itself. While he is considered fundamentally a monist, he saw that emphasis on the One had ended up in the subordination of the many, and the hegemony of the absolute and the logical over the relative and the sensate. Heraclitean thought was a rejection of this, an attempt to restore the balance between the One and the many, and the rejection of logic in favour of the world of sense. This occurs through understanding process, acknowledging that 'Out of all things [comes] one thing, and out of one thing all things.'[2] Heraclitus' emphasis is always on change rather than on things themselves. In his well-known statement that you can never step into the same river twice, there is the paradoxical acknowledgement of the identity of the process and the change of the material. In a manner that foreshadows the idea of the two truths and resonates with ideas of emptiness in Buddhism, he stated: 'We are and are not', and also:

> God [is] day [and] night, winter [and] summer, war [and] peace, satiety [and] famine, and undergoes change in the way that [fire?], whenever it is mixed with spices, gets called by the name that accords with [the] bouquet of each.[3]

He also said that 'Fullness and emptiness are the same thing.'[4]

French philosopher Marcel Conche speaks of the similarity of Heraclitean and Taoist thought, while the resonance of such statements with the teachings of Buddhism are particularly noted by Thomas McEvilley, who undertook the most extraordinarily thorough and wide-ranging exploration of the history, matter and diffusion of early Eastern and Western philosophy in his amazing book *The Shape of Ancient Thought* (2002), to which I am much indebted in this chapter. He notes that Heraclitus' response to the monism of Xenophanes is similar to that of Early Buddhists to Upanisadic monism. McEvilley states that the concept of a state of being that is beyond or prior to qualities is the first purely philosophical idea, and one that evolved through the progressive stripping away of concrete imagery of the Cosmic Person, or God. Furthermore, he points out that there are pre-echoes of Madhyamaka thought. Before the fact, Heraclitus rejects the three classical laws of thought: the Law of Identity (that A is A and not not-A), the Law of Non-contradiction (that nothing can be both A and not-A at the same time) and the Law of Excluded Middle (that every entity must be A or not-A) in a manner that we have seen in the dialectic of Nagarjuna. McEvilley also notes direct parallels between Heraclitean ideas and images and those in

Vedic and Upanisadic texts, particularly those in relation to fire. Such thinking was the basis for the later schools of Cynicism and Pyrrhonism.

After Heraclitus, Democritus, the father of atomism, undertook the task of rescuing plurality and the senses from the hegemony of monism and mind. According to Democritus the distinction between truth and appearance is not a religious one but a naturalistic one: not a dichotomy between the point of view of the divine and the human, but one between evidence of the senses and deduction. Our subjectivity veils us from real information: sweet and sour, and colour and so forth, exist only by convention; 'in reality there is only atoms and void'. On the other hand, Democritus held that the qualities that we seem to perceive are an accurate picture of the result of the mixture of our senses with those unseen atoms, and thus, in terms of us as receivers, they are true, so accepting that appearance is reality. His ethics were centred on the desirability of the inability to be disturbed (ataraxia), and McEvilly suggests that many of Democritus' ethical pronouncements could equally have been made by the Buddha.

This ethical or eudaemonist intention to promote well-being by the seeking of quietude is a hallmark of the schools of Greek thought that resonates with the topic of emptiness. This was a project that was shared by Stoics, Sceptics and Epicureans, the last of whom, despite the reputation that has come from the use of their name in later times to denote lovers of hedonistic pleasure, actually sought the absence of pain, which they felt came largely from misplaced beliefs. This concern with beliefs was shared by the Sceptics, particularly those of the Pyrrhonist tradition.

McEvilley delineates great similarity in content, intention and method between the teachings of Pyrrho, who lived in the fourth century BC and whose philosophy was expanded by Sextus Empiricus in the second century AD, and Buddhist teachings. Another book, *Pyrrhonism* by Adrian Kuzminski, subtitled *How the Ancient Greeks Reinvented Buddhism*, also describes the similarities between the philosophies. Indeed, Kuzminski emphasizes that Pyrrhonism was not a view, theory or belief, but pre-eminently a therapeutic practice whose aim was a way to live with an easy, untroubled mind. This was to be achieved not by establishing any form of conceptual foundation for knowledge or truth, but by refusing to hold beliefs about non-evident matters. Kuzminski makes the claim that Pyrrhonism has been misguidedly interpreted by later writers in terms of dogmatic scepticism, which moved from doubt as a tool of inquiry to doubt as an end in itself, thus paradoxically embracing doubt as belief, which would amount, in Nagarjuna's terms, to mishandling the snake.

Pyrrho's teaching was that beliefs about non-evident matters cannot be substantiated and must remain unstable and open to challenge by competing beliefs, and thus be the cause of suffering and anxiety due to lack of certainty. Such beliefs should be avoided by suspending judgement (*epoché*) about claims that go beyond present or possible immediate experience. The liberation from anxiety brought about by such suspension of judgement is ataraxia.

According to Kuzminski, Pyrrho accepted evident matters, regarding detachment and indifference as the correct response only to non-evident matters. What is evident is taken to be immediate involuntary experience, called 'appearances', which include both sensations and thoughts, and which are to be accepted at face value. Thus liberation is offered not only by removing

> the problematic burden of defending some non-evident dogmatic belief, but also because it allows us to respond to our direct experience of objects without distortions, excesses and denials introduced by unsubstantiated beliefs about those objects.[5]

This is very similar to the Buddhist teaching: 'Understanding based on apprehension by any one of the six unimpaired faculties is true by the standard of everyday experience, while any remaining concepts are false according to this same criterion.'[6] Pyrronhism and Buddhism both accept the five traditional senses, plus a sixth, or mental, sense, concerned with thoughts as objects of memory or imagination. Appearances are what is given directly in our experience, unmediated through concepts; they are not abstractions. They are both self-evident and empty, or without underlying nature; 'more than appearances is neither given nor required'.[7] Appearances, involuntary objects of consciousness, both sensations and thoughts, are to be taken and explained in their own terms; any abstractions of essences, categories or concepts on top of this would be a belief in the independent existence of a non-evident object. As Kuzminski says:

> the ever-shocking doubt of the independent existence of the external world is perhaps the Pyrrhonist's most notorious observation. The Pyrrhonists suspend judgment because they can find nothing evident, that is, no object of consciousness, which fulfills the claim that our purportedly internal appearances actually represent externally existing objects that constitute their reality.[8]

Pyrrhonian relativity may be compared to Buddhist dependent origination. Thus experience without belief might be likened to the *skandhas* (psychophysical aggregates) without attachment – both are just the working of the world, as it is, the result of dependent origination. Liberation from beliefs and opinions, whether it be termed ataraxia or nirvana, is the end of wilful activity, an addition of distorting interpretations, theories or beliefs on to experience. What is left is pure experience.

The more our beliefs are winnowed out from our appearances, the more our appearances stand forth just as they are, freed of the distortions imposed by our beliefs about them. The more we suspend judgment about beliefs the more we live in the real world of appearances.[9]

The most radical exposition of the thought of Pyrrho comes from Conche. However, he had forerunners in understanding the radical overthrow of foundations, the understanding of emptiness that Pyrrho experienced. Conche quotes Nietzsche, writing, 'Although a Greek, [Pyrrho] was a Buddhist, even a Buddha', and continues in his own voice, 'Yes, Pyrrho is 'Buddhist', but Greek. That is, Buddhist but with irony.'[10] According to Conche, Pyrrho presented a radical attack on the foundations implicit in all Western metaphysics: the idea of being. Yet at the same time,

the *nothing* [*rien*] at which Pyrrho arrives is a completely other *nothing* than the nothingness [*néant*] which would simply be the opposite of being. For each thing, one can no more say 'it is' than 'it is not'. And no more 'it is not' than 'it is' . . . For the Pyrhonist *nothing* is neither pure nothingness nor non-being. One can call it *appearance*.[11]

All foundation and essence are disallowed, allowing only that all is appearance: 'Appearance, wherever it presents itself, extends to everything.' It is, however, a pure and universal appearance that implies neither appearance-of nor appearance-for, which might imply the existence of either the object that appears or the subject to whom something appears.

Conche's careful exposition of Pyrrhonian thought, which distinguishes it from later accretions of dogmatism or phenomenism, relies on two texts, one by Aristocles, quoted by Eusebius, relating to Pyrrho's disciple Timon of Phlius, the other by Aenesidemus. According to the first:

According to Timon, Pyrrho declared that all things are equally in-different, un-measurable and un-decidable. Therefore neither our sensations nor our opinions tell us truth or falsehoods.

Therefore, we should not put the slightest trust in them, but be without judgement, without preference, and unwavering, saying about each thing that is no more is than is not, or both is and is not or neither is or is not.[12]

Pyrronhism is the radical extension of the *ou mallon*, or the 'no more' this than that, which erases all difference and all essence. It is common experience that reifies beings, and a metaphysic of being lies on this foundation of common sense that Pyrrho radically undermines. Pyrrhonism, like Buddhism, requires a transition in view from being to appearance. What remains is appearance, pure and simple, 'in-different, un-measurable and un-decidable'. Yet such unknowing does not leave us in a state of privation compared with the 'riches of Being; on the contrary it is within un-knowing that things open themselves and expose themselves without anything hidden and without any foundation, that is to say, as appearances'.[13]

Thus we can see many similarities between Buddhist Madhyamaka thought, the home of a philosophy of emptiness, and Greek Pyrrhonian Scepticism. Neither claimed to propound a doctrine; both taught that appearances were phenomenally real, and neither posited that they were real essentially. Both upheld the idea of a double truth: an absolute truth, and a relative or conventional truth. The first is the truth of emptiness, according to which phenomena are no more true than false, real than unreal; the second is that truth in the light of which inductive statements based on direct experience and observation may be treated as valid for the purpose of making distinctions to guide everyday life.

Methodically, both schools taught by undermining the arguments of others rather than offering positive doctrines of their own. Both espoused a soteriological intention; the Sceptic practitioner intended to bring his mind into a state of suspension, an inner balance of equanimity in which the mind neither affirms nor denies, striving only for imperturbability in which the mind can experience each moment freed from attachment or aversion. Similarly, the Buddhist intention is to quiet the mind and avoid conceptual proliferation (*prapanca*), which leads to dispositions of grasping and aversion. As a sage is described in one of the earliest texts, the Sutta Nipata, without 'the least preconceived perception with regard to what is seen, heard or sensed'.[14]

Both schools adopt the middle position and may be said to negate the Law of Excluded Middle, critiquing claims both of being and non-being. They both use the tetralemma, or catuskoti, a four-pointed logic that expands logical possibility from simply P or not-P to include both P and not-P, and neither P nor not-P, as we saw in the work of Nagarjuna. He stated that: 'One should say of each thing that it neither is, nor is not, nor both is and is not, nor neither is or is not', and Pyrrho reportedly stated: 'We should . . . [say] of each thing that it no more is than is not, than both is and is not, than neither is nor is not.'[15] McEvilley cites passages from both Buddhist and Sceptic writings to illustrate that both reject the Law of Excluded Middle as 'an ethical and psychological factor associated with relativity and subjectivity'. He sees both the Greek *aoristia* (lack of boundary or definition) and the Sanskrit *sunyata* (lack of self-nature or essence) as 'the doctrine of indeterminacy', and as being

> simultaneously a critique of ontological claims of absolute Being or non-Being, or epistemological claims for knowledge, and of the view that there is a language–reality isomorphism.[16]

The dialectic used, as pointed out by McEvilley, works on three levels: ontological, epistemological and semantic. For both the dialectic is ultimately self-destroying – in Buddhist terms in the emptiness of emptiness, in the Sceptic in the suspension of doubt as a method without the positing of doubt as an end. In the words of Nagarjuna: 'Nothing could be asserted to be sunya, asunya, both sunya and asunya, and neither sunya or asunya. They are asserted only for the purpose of provisional understanding.' According to Sextus Empiricus, the dialectic 'is like fire, which, after consuming the fuel, destroys itself also'.[17]

If the similarities of Pyrrhonian Scepticism are mostly with the Madhyamaka, McEvilley also finds similarities between Early Buddhism, Epicureanism and Stoicism in terms of naturalistic theories of knowledge based on sense experience, naturalistic doctrines of causality, a fundamentally naturalistic ethics based on pleasure and pain rather than absolute good or evil, a naturalistic psychology and, based on this, their strategies for what he calls 'interrupting mental process'. This is the manner in which they advocate mindfulness that may de-link or defer the process of perception and action in order to foster considered response to a stimulus rather than unconsidered reaction. It is this understanding that I believe has made dialogue between Buddhist thought and psychology, particularly psychotherapy, so important in the contemporary world. I do not think that such understanding in Greek thought has been as well documented, perhaps due to the lack of existent formal awareness practices. In Western thought, where over the centuries theory was increasingly separated from experiential practice, traditions of practice have died out and today we have turned to the still-flourishing Eastern traditions.

The intention is to gain self-mastery and non-reactiveness, to bring one's own mind – that over which one may have some control – into alignment with the flow of events, with the impermanence and unsatisfactoriness of the world over which we have no control. Mindfulness promotes careful introspective examination of mental processes, without interpretation and evaluation. McEvilley suggests that Stoic ethics may be more like Early Buddhist ones than those of any other Western system, and that moreover 'Epicureanism may be even more like early Buddhism than Stoicism is.'[18] He also notes a similarity between the ethics and epistemology of the Cynics and Buddhism – the first in that the test of action is to find out whether or not it leads to detachment or attachment, and the second in the way concepts and strivings are seen to be like 'smoke' in their common attacks on linguistic reification.

The path to quietude, to the elimination of concepts, involves a direct relationship with the present moment. In Buddhist teaching this comes through the path of mindfulness and meditation. The Greek teachings are similar to mindfulness in their emphasis on a non-conceptual, non-judgemental awareness of the present moment. The Greeks also believed that much depends on training the mind and on practices. If McEvilley and Kuzminski have elucidated the similarities of content between Hellenstic and Eastern traditions, Pierre Hadot has done the same for practices.

If no traditions of what we might call meditation practices have come down to us from the ancient Greeks, there most certainly did exist practices of imagination and thought experiments. Meditation in their case, according to Hadot, was 'the exercise of reason'. Unlike Buddhist practice it has no somatic content, 'but is a purely rational, imaginative, or intuitive exercise that can take extremely varied forms'.[19] He mentions memorization of the dogmas and rules of the schools, and imaginative practices such as the Epicurean contemplation of the genesis of worlds and the Stoic contemplation of the unfolding of cosmic events, both of which give a perspective to the small space occupied by human concerns. He mentions particularly meditation on death and the attentive concentration on the present moment in order to live with full awareness and enjoyment. At this time, Hadot tells us, theory was not considered an end in itself, but was always clearly placed in the service of practice. Each school, he says, had its own therapeutic method, but all of them were in the service of the transformation of the practitioner's mode of seeing and being.[20] Indeed, the term 'theory' referred initially to a form of contemplation, a 'looking at', without expectation or judgement. In the Orthodox Christian tradition a method of prayer akin to meditation still exists.

What all these similarities of teaching demonstrate is that consideration of the Western, Greek heritage with an unawareness of Indian thought can no longer be upheld. How and when diffusion occurred is still a subject of much dispute and outside our concern here. McEvilley believes that teachings about monism and the Heraclitean view of process were directly influenced by the Upanishads, thus showing Indian influence in the Presocratic era, but that in the Indian tradition, the formalization of the dialectic, as shown in the Madhyamaka, represents Greek influence back to India in the Hellenistic era. Here Kuzminski disagrees. He suggests that Pyrrho, who is known to have accompanied Alexander the Great on his expedition to India, brought his teachings back with him, while McEvilley suggests that the methods used by the Madhyamaka dialectic could be traced back several centuries earlier in Greece.

Such disagreement is not of relevance here. What is indisputable is that early periods of Greek and Indian philosophy demonstrate many shared elements. Among those most relevant to my philosophical exploration of emptiness are consideration of the One and the many; the emergence of a category of formlessness alongside that of form, and their union in immanent-transcendent process; consideration of indeterminacy; and a therapeutic intent that was the foundation for tangible practices.

# FIVE

# Philosophic Modernity

The search for something permanent is one of the deepest
of the instincts leading men to philosophy.
Bertrand Russell

We have traced philosophic concern with emptiness from the
East, with Buddhist and Taoist thought, and travelled west with
the Greeks with possible counterinfluence from Greece on later
Indian theories. This diffusion of influence eventually came to
an end and the philosophies, and in particular the practices of
emptiness, faded in the West. After the coming of Christianity
its echoes died away for many centuries, while emptiness came
to be considered as mere privation of God and faith, both of
which stood as bulwarks against contingency, as providers of
permanence.

In the first chapter of Genesis, God creates the world, and
imposes division and meaning upon the Void. 'In the beginning
God created the heaven and the earth. And the earth was without form, and void; and darkness was on the face of the deep.'
The Void was not the source but a privative chaos before God.

The Greek voices that proposed metaphysics of presence
and transcendence, separating ideal forms from living matter,
were those heard the loudest; others, those most concerned
with emptiness, were muted and forgotten. Furthermore, there
was a separation of theory from practice. Philosophy lost its
function as the foundation of a way of life and became what

Pierre Hadot has called philosophical discourse. Practice remained only in the contemplation and prayer of monastics, while theories (the very word having lost the embodied and contemplative aspect of its meaning) were discussed and disputed in the academies. Yet some echoes of emptiness still faintly resonated, most often in the writings of mystics, the singers of what we would today call negative theology and the apophatic voice. They differ from the expressions of emptiness that we have considered heretofore in that they do reflect a belief in some form of transcendence, God or a godhead, that certainly Buddhist thought is without. Yet the reflections of emptiness are, I think, sufficient to merit notice of them here.

The echoes consist philosophically of the strands of thought concerning the relationship of everything and nothing, the understanding of emptiness as potential, and the difficulties of speaking of what is ineffable: in practice they centre around the idea of *kenosis*. Kenosis comes from the Greek word for emptiness and refers to the practice of emptying all traces of self-will from the mind of the practitioner so that it may be filled with God.

A work concerning the discourses of negative theology, of what the author terms 'unsaying', begins by pointing to Eastern texts such as the Tao-te-Ching with its 'Tao that can be spoken as not the true Tao, and the Buddhist understanding that all concepts are empty including the emptiness of emptiness itself, as examples of apophasis'.[1] The writer suggests that apophasis, description by negation, appears in many places and within many traditions – Islamic, Jewish and Christian – but does not typically form into schools. I would suggest that it is usually the result of individual contemplation and practice. It is also often outside the major traditions of its time, and its expression frequently brings to its adherents accusations of heresy. For apophasis is a discourse similar to that of Buddhism and the Madhyamaka, in which any single proposition is seen as reifying and falsifying the way things truly are. It is a dialectic of saying and unsaying, of immanence and transcendence, which ultimately is performative and has the aim of leading to realization.

The names associated with apophatic writings are those of individuals, rather than schools. There are many that could be mentioned here, but I shall merely refer to a few and consider even fewer in any detail. The first I shall mention is Plotinus, who lived in Alexandria in the third century AD and was known to have travelled beyond Europe and studied Eastern philosophy. Then came Dionysius the Areopagite, a somewhat mysterious figure who became an important influence on this type of thought in the Western tradition, with his expressions of mystical theology and *agnosia*, unknowing. In particular, he influenced John Scotus Erigena, who translated his work, the unknown author of *The Cloud of Unknowing* and Meister Eckhart.

John Scotus Erigena in the ninth century AD combined the Dionysian affirmation that deity is beyond being with the apparently startling claim that *dies nihil est*, God is nothing. His understanding of the relationship between everything and nothing, however, is clearly expressed in the following excerpt:

> But when I hear or say that the divine good created all from nothing, I do not understand what is signified by that name, 'nothing', whether the privation of all essence or substance or accident, or the excellence of the divine beyond-essence.[2]

Such an understanding of the emptiness beyond the limitation of signification is also expressed by Eckhart, who is regularly referenced in discussions of mystical theology for his breathtaking sayings such as, 'The eye with which I see God is the same eye with which God sees me'. Arthur Schopenhauer likened Eckhart to Sakyamuni Buddha (as also have D. T.

Suzuki and Rudolf Otto), in the sense that he saw the Godhead as pure nothingness beyond God, saying that the *istigkeit* (isness) of God is a negation of all quiddity, and that deity, as empty of finite existence – negation of negation – is fullness of being. He wrote: 'If the heart is to find preparedness for the highest of all flights, it must aim at pure nothing, and in this there is the greatest possibility that can exist.'[3] Such paradoxical understanding may explain why in the twentieth century Jacques Derrida turned back to Eckhart's negative theology to describe his concept of *différance*.[4]

Eckhart's words remind me of the writing of the thirteenth-century Japanese Buddhist Dōgen, in terms of the difficulty of expressing within language what transcends our conventional meaning, pointing to what stands before language, category, time and convention:

> When I still stood in my first cause, there I had no God and was cause of myself. There I willed nothing, I desired nothing, for I was a pure being and a knower of myself in delight of the truth. There I willed myself and nothing else. What I willed, that I was; and what I was, that I willed. There I stood, free of God and of all things. But when I took leave from this state of free will and received my created being, then I had a God. Indeed before creatures were, God was not yet 'God'; rather he was what he was. But when creatures came to be and when they received their created being the God was no longer 'God' in himself, rather, he was 'God' in the creatures.[5]

Eckhart understood that to be full of God, one needs to let go of willing and seek the solitude within. *Gelassenheit*, 'releasement' or 'letting-go', which reappears centuries later in the philosophy of Martin Heidegger, is a central term in the writings of Eckhart. One must become, in Eckhart's words, a 'poor

person' who 'is one who wills nothing and desires nothing . . .
People should stand empty.'[6] Eckhart suggests that

> a person must be so poor that he or she is no place and
> has no place wherein God could act. Where people still
> preserve some place in themselves, they preserve distinc-
> tion. This is why I pray God to rid me of God; for my
> essential being is above God as the origin of creatures.
> Indeed, in God's own being, where God is raised above
> all being and all distinctions, there I was myself, there I
> willed myself, and I knew myself to create this person
> that I am. Therefore I am cause of myself according to
> my being, which is eternal, but not according to my
> becoming, which is temporal. There also I am unborn
> and following the way of my unborn being I have always
> been, I am now, and shall remain eternally.

Realizing the difficulty of his words and thoughts, Eckhart
stated that if anyone could not understand this discourse they
should not trouble their hearts about it, for as long as they do
not equal this truth, they would not understand this speech.

Kenosis, or emptying of the mind and the will, is also found
in the writing of St John of the Cross and the Illuminists in
the early sixteenth century in Castile, which encourages letting
go and surrender to the love of God. Indeed, St John of the
Cross has been called *el doctor de nada* (the doctor of nothing)
possibly for such lines as:

> I entered in, not knowing where
> And there remained, unknowing
> All knowledge transcending[7]

In another text, 'Ascent of Mount Carmel', St John expressed
the paradoxical relationship between everything and nothing

in lines that T. S. Eliot, in some ways another Christian mystic, drew on in 'East Coker', from his 'Four Quartets':

To achieve pleasure in everything
You must take pleasure in nothing

. . . In order to know everything
You must seek to know nothing

. . . To reach what you do not know
You must go through the way of unknowing

. . . In order to reach what you are not
You must go through the way of unbeing[8]

The Lutheran theologian Jakob Böhme (1575–1624) also touches emptiness, speaking of the '*Ungrund*', or unground, as an indefinable matrix out of which everything arises. Again, it is self-will that is seen as enclosing us and preventing us from participation. Again, the letting-go of *Gelassenheit* and the putting-to-the-side of *epoché* are necessary to provide methods of releasing such enclosure.

The list of mystical opponents (for they were always individuals rather than a tradition) to the hegemony of the Church weakens from the eighteenth century. After the Enlightenment and the Industrial Revolution, alternative views were more a reaction to reason and the scientific rationalization of nature, the new guarantors of permanence, than to religious dogma, and came from artists rather than the religious, appearing in the uprush of Romanticism.

When Bertrand Russell wrote his telling words concerning the search for permanence as the source of philosophy, he illustrated a lack of consideration for any but Western philosophy, a trait that is still found today. Yet the certainties and the permanence sought were, when he wrote, becoming harder to find, whether in religion or in science. Entering into modernity, the centuries of Christian hegemony, first questioned by the Enlightenment, were over, and practitioners in science, philosophy, politics and the arts attacked old certainties. Echoes of emptiness and ambiguity, long withstood, re-entered philosophic discourse, slowly and incrementally, until the landscape significantly changed. Nietzsche proclaimed the death of God, Darwin's theory of evolution questioned the literal truth of creation, and Freud questioned the stability and authority of the conscious self. The *Oxford English Dictionary* defines metaphysics as 'that branch of speculative inquiry which treats of the first principles of things, including such concepts as being, substance, essence, time, space, cause, identity etc.' Thus, as traditionally conceived, metaphysics is concerned with first principles; the separation of essence and existence, of ground and becoming. Little wonder, then, that by the twentieth century Heidegger spoke of the end of metaphysics and Derrida of the end of ontotheology; for the end of metaphysics is the end of the privilege of presence and first principle – self-presence – sure of its ground. Such journeys, however, lead into new territory, away from nouns and things on a path of process and verbs that is more often found among Eastern philosophies and ideas of emptiness.

As modernism turned into postmodernism, its theme continued along the lines of Jean-François Lyotard's oft-quoted 'incredulity towards metanarratives'. *Différance*, decentralization, deconstruction and distributed views of self are the tropes of contemporary philosophy that trawl in their wake suggestions of emptiness of essence, interdependence and interaction.

In times of change, when traditional foundations are weakened or destroyed, there are three main choices: first, to find other foundations, which may even be a belief in unbelief, as in extreme scepticism, nihilism and atheism, even while knowing that this new view may be as susceptible to change as previous ones; second, in the face of all evidence to ignore new knowledge and turn to faith to support a literal and fundamentalist support for the old beliefs; or third, to place change and impermanence themselves at the centre of philosophy. A philosophy of emptiness is obviously that of the third choice.

In tracing echoes of indeterminacy and emptiness in modernist thought, there are many steps and turns and brief encounters, some of which I shall attempt to follow. If we look at almost any discipline of the last hundred years or so, we find a movement towards notions of loss of essential authority, indeterminacy, contingency and immanence. In every branch of human endeavour we will find resonance of emptiness. Exploring this today, we are looking not at one school of philosophy or practice with the hindsight of long history, but at individual attempts to become more aware and make sense of emptiness, revealed as earlier defences against contingency, gods and theories, falter. Thus the text inevitably becomes more varied; perhaps more contingent itself, as paths diverge through the empty terrain, with the danger of becoming mere lists of disparate narratives. Yet there is a theme: the response to emptiness. As this is experiential rather than theoretical, so there will be different responses ranging through different emotions, from horror to freedom. Everyone to whom this is of any interest will surely have their own favoured examples. I shall attempt to explore some of mine. I intend to consider discipline by discipline but there will inevitably be much blurring of boundaries between disciplines as such overlap has been a feature of the zeitgeist. In particular we will often find philosophy, art, psychology and, more recently, neuroscience meeting in practices of attention.

One thread exists that attempts to bring philosophy back from theory closer to lived experience. Such philosophy, in the pragmatist philosopher Richard Rorty's terms, is edifying rather than systematic. Kant had first set in motion the loss of the object, the thing in itself which exists independent of experience; then phenomenological thought began the return to subjectivity; later, Existentialism foregrounded existence before essence. Later still, a close attention, even a deconstruction, paid to language, perception and writing, began to expose the conventionality and relativity of our categories of thought and language. The lenses of the spectacles worn for centuries were being cleansed. As science and psychology exposed the constructed nature of the self, so the barriers between self and world also came down, and philosophy has concerned itself with this dependence. Thus another line of development traces an expanding arc beyond the subject into its context, and beyond fixed presence or truth into a wider field. As one commentator noted, 'continental philosophy operates in terms of an orientation towards openness.'[9]

In the first existential response, the human being is, in Heidegger's term, 'already thrown' into the world. She is Dasein, being there. Is this thrownness meaningful or a buzzing confusion without meaning that induces the nausea of Sartre's Roquentin or Kundera's *unbearable* lightness of being? As Karl Jaspers described it,

What makes us afraid is our great freedom, in face of the emptiness that is still to be filled . . . The philosophically serious European is faced today with the choice between opposed philosophical possibilities. Will he enter the limited field of fixed truth which in the end has only to be obeyed, or will he go into the limitless open truth?[10]

Also:

Once I envision world history or life's entirety as a kind of finite totality I can act only on the basis of sham knowledge, in distortion of actual possibilities, far from reality . . . Whenever my knowledge is chained to total concepts, whenever my actions are based on a specific world-view, I am distracted from what I am really able to do. I am cheated of the present . . . for the sake of something imagined (past or future) rather than real, which has not been actually lived and has never been realized.[11]

Recent philosophy has attempted to move away from totality into an exploration of reality and the linguistic practice that was thought to describe and encompass it but which, we now see, may help to create it.

In his first and only work published in his lifetime, Ludwig Wittgenstein showed that the problems of meaning in life transcended the limits of language, and that claims about self, death and the meaning of life lay outside what can be logically stated. 'What we cannot speak about we must pass over in silence', he wrote, stating also:

My work consists in two parts – the one presented here plus all that I have *not* written. And it is precisely this second part that is the important one . . . In short, I believe that where *many* others today are just *gassing*, I have managed in my book to put everything firmly in place by being silent about it.[12]

In his later *Philosophical Investigations*, Wittgenstein continued exploring the way language is embedded in forms of life. His aim was therapeutic, to let the 'fly out of the fly bottle', as he put it. One of the problems he saw was the 'bewitchment' of language: how we become caught in the inevitable reification of words and the objective truth of the world as presented in language. In opposition to this, Wittgenstein presents us with a realm of language games, founded not on privileged transcendental standards but dependent merely on a context of conventional cultural and historical criteria – the rules of the game. Understanding that language is merely conventionally true, may release us from its grip. Such argument trails traces of Nagarjuna. Moreover, Wittgenstein, emphasizing his therapeutic intention, says, 'Giving grounds [must] come to an end sometime. But the end is not in ungrounded presupposition: it is an ungrounded way of acting.'[13]

If Wittgenstein pointed to the emptiness of silence and the contingency of language, Heidegger, in very different form, was concerned with the interface of beings and being in a way that highlights the concept of openness. As we saw, it begins with Dasein, being there, which from the very start brings subject and context together, *being* and *there*. Being-in-the-world is a relationship that is prior to all scientific conceptualization, to all emotional experience, being the fundamental relatedness of the human being to what is. This presupposes an openness to man's existence compared to which our normative divisions into subject and object may be considered a deficient mode of being-in-the-world.

> Being essentially self-interpreting, Dasein has no nature. Yet Dasein always understands itself as having some specific essential nature, and feels at home in belonging to a certain nation or a certain race. Thus Dasein's everyday pre-ontological understanding of its own being necessarily involved a pre-ontological misunderstanding. Understanding itself thus as an object with a fixed essence covers up Dasein's unsettledness and calms the anxiety occasioned by recognizing that Dasein is interpretation all the way down.[14]

This encompasses both Dasein's actual emptiness of essence and the emotional anxiety caused by this. To approach life from the perspective of a fixed ego is a restriction of the openness in which Dasein exists. The task is to face anxiety and death with resoluteness, the word for which, in German, contains a pun on unclosedness, openness to being.

Heidegger's later work was concerned with this relationship of beings to being, and he saw that to deal with this meant the end of 'metaphysics' into a new mode of enquiry he called 'thinking' that is close to thanking. This is an attempt, close to poetic endeavour, to see matters in a new light that is open and evades the dualities inherent in philosophies of presence.

> What characterizes metaphysical thinking, which investigates the ground for being, is that such thinking, starting from what is present, represents it in its presence and thus exhibits it as grounded by its ground.[15]

Heidegger depicted the contemporary world as one in which there has never been greater subjectivism, which in turn elicits an objectivism, an impoverishment of the world seen as representation in which everything is understood from the perspective of man. This he saw as the problem of technological thinking implicit in the act of 'framing', in which thinking is represented and calculated in terms of its usage. It was to counter this that he advocated this new kind of thought, *Andenken* or *Besinnung*, usually translated as meditative thinking or remembrance. Such thought is evoked by *Gelassenheit*, letting-go, a term that was also used by Meister Eckhart.

A similar act or non-act concerns speech; Heidegger seeks a transformation of speech beginning in the 'ringing of stillness' (*das Galäut de Stille*), which seems almost more a matter of hearing differently than speaking differently. Again it is a change from a position of mastery to one of receptivity, which he calls a transformation from speech to saying, in which to say means to let appear, to show. Such saying is a response, a dwelling within saying as the house of being, rather than speech that merely designates. It is another step into the open. It also reminds me of a distinction made by the poet Alice Oswald between prose and poetry: poetry includes silence.[16] It is no coincidence that Heidegger's later work often enters into the world of poetry, as writing and as commentary.

Heidegger's struggle was to think what it was in the relationship of beings to being that remained unthought. His path backwards from beings to Being led him to somewhere (not something) not unlike an emptiness that is also neither empty nor unmoving, but an ungrounded arising of being. Ways to access this state also imply practices of thought similar to mindful awareness and contemplation. The similarities of this to Eastern thinking have been increasingly noticed. Recent research has shown that Heidegger had a far greater familiarity with Eastern thought than he commonly acknowledged in his writings. Apart from his association with several Japanese students and friends, he had started a translation of the Tao-te-Ching, and was also familiar with the work of D. T. Suzuki, whose translations and commentaries were largely responsible for the dissemination of Zen Buddhism in the West.[17] It has been suggested that his reticence in acknowledging such works as influential came from his unfamiliarity with the original languages of such texts.

The works that most embody these echoes of emptiness are those that Heidegger wrote as dialogues between two or three participants. The earliest translated into English was 'A Dialogue on Language', which appeared in 1971 as part of *On the Way to Language*. More recently this has been republished along with two other dialogues as *Country Path Conversations*. Here we find much that is resonant with a philosophy of emptiness; indeed it is only, as a Japanese commentator noted, within an understanding of emptiness that it can be properly understood. Speaking of a Japanese translation of Heidegger's *What is Metaphysics?*, the Japanese commentator marvels

> to this day how the Europeans could lapse into interpreting as nihilistic the nothingness of which you speak in that lecture. To us, emptiness is the loftiest name for what you mean to say with the word 'Being'.[18]

Throughout these dialogues there occur references to emptiness that resound with the thought of Buddhism and Taoism. There is an indication of the idea of emptiness as origin: 'The jug consists not in the piece of formed earth but in its emptiness; the potter does not shape the clay, but rather the emptiness.' And again: 'Emptiness is the ungraspable.'[19]

Similarly, the other face of emptiness, dependent origination, also appears:

> The drink abides in the whole gathering involved in the event of drinking. This gathering is the belonging-together in the event of drinking of what is offered and received as drinkable. The whole gathering of the drink consists of the drink offered and the drink received. What is offered as drinkable is among other things wine. The one who drinks is the human. The whole gathering of the drink as what is offered abides in the wine, which abides in the grapevine, which abides in the earth and in the gifts from the sky.

To which the scholar responds: 'So the emptiness of the jug is brought to abide in such an expanse. This expanse is what brings the jug to abide in resting in this return to itself.'[20]

To attain to this thinking/thanking requires releasement and a non-willing that is reminiscent of the *wu wei* of Taoism and, as noted earlier, uses the same term *Gelassenheit* in much the same manner as it was employed by Meister Eckhart. As the latter stated, 'one must let go of, release God, for the sake of God', so in Heidegger's words we have, 'Thinking is releasement to the open-region . . . When we let ourselves engage in releasement to the open-region, we will not-willing.'[21]

In a dialogue between an Inquirer (designated as I) and a Japanese (J), speaking of Noh plays, the Inquirer notes that the emptiness of the empty stage demands concentration; the Japanese responds that thanks to that concentration only a slight gesture by an actor is needed 'to cause mighty things to appear out of a strange stillness'. The essence of this gesture they discuss in dialogue is a beholding that 'is itself invisible, and that, so gathered, bears itself to encounter emptiness in such a way that in and through it the mountains open'.[22] So within concentration, only a 'slight gesture' is necessary to enter the open that is consonant with emptiness and being. 'That emptiness', says the Inquirer, 'is the same as nothingness, that essential being which we attempt to add in our thinking, as the open, to all that is present or absent'.[23] And:

> We are not and are never outside the open-region, insofar as we stay, after all, as thinking beings – and that means as transcendental representing beings – in the horizon of transcendence. The horizon, however, is the side of the open-region turned towards our representational setting-before. The open-region surrounds us and shows itself to us as the horizon.[24]

This is the distinction between the open and our representational 'setting-before', the objectification of nature that is the technological stance.

> Accordingly, we may suggest that the day will come when we will not shun the question whether the clearing, the free

open, may not be that within which alone pure space and ecstatic time and everything present and absent in them have their place which gather and shelters everything.[25]

Such quotations should be an answer to the Western tendency, referred to by the Japanese commentator above, to see any questioning of presence as absence, an absence that can lead only to nihilism. This shadow of nihilism is something that has been of supreme concern since Nietzsche, who defined it as the devaluation of the highest values.

As Heidegger was influenced by Eastern thinking, his work was also influential in contemporary Japanese philosophy, especially for the so-called Kyoto School of philosophers, some members of which actually studied with him in Germany. Nishitani Keiji grasps the problem of nihilism head-on and argues that nihilism or relative nothingness is a necessary step in the process of understanding and accepting emptiness, which is absolute nothing. In his major work, *Religion and Nothingness*, he states that: 'the overcoming of this pessimistic nihilism represents the single greatest issue facing philosophy and religion in our times.'[26] Nishitani argues that in modern times the essence of human existence has become identified with self-consciousness, so that we see ourselves only according to the horizons of what he terms the 'field of consciousness'. He sees a necessary trajectory from the field of consciousness *through* the field of relative nihility to the field of absolute nothingness beyond all duality, which is that of emptiness, *sunyata*. 'The standpoint of emptiness is altogether different: it is an absolute openness.'[27]

The move from the field of self-consciousness into the field of nihility is a moment of conversion from the egoic or anthropocentric mode of being, which asks what use things have for us, to an attitude which questions the meaning and intention of ourselves, so that 'existence itself then turns into a single great question mark'.[28] The next step leads from this field of nihility, which Nishitani considers a relative nothingness still tainted with representation, to the field of *sunyata*, of absolute nothingness, which is one with absolute being. There is an echo of these steps in Heidegger's writing: '[To] put in question our own being so that it becomes questionable in its relatedness to Being, and thereby open to Being.'[29] Both also carry traces of Eckhart's writing of God and godhead.

A Buddhist writer suggested that from a Buddhist perspective, the contemporary view of the contingency, relativity and plurality of things, with its unwillingness to admit of any transcendent category beyond the process of diffusion, is comparable to talking about dependent origination without the concept of emptiness, a source that goes beyond categories of presence and absence.[30]

Derrida might perhaps be considered from this standpoint. A key term in his discourse is that of *différance*, which stands for the impossibility and continual deferring of self-identity in a manner similar to dependent origination. Like emptiness, *différance* itself has no absolute existence:

> Différance is not. It is not a present being, however excellent, unique, principal or transcendent. It governs nothing, reigns over nothing and nowhere exercises any authority . . . not only is there no kingdom of différance, but différance instigates the subversion of every kingdom, which makes it obviously threatening and infallibly dreaded by everything within us that desires a kingdom, the past or future presence of a kingdom.[31]

Derrida shows that in the lack of a direct relation of signifier and signified, the sign is a structure of difference that is defined as much by what it is not as by what it is. Thus meaning is to be found in the spaces between. Every sign carries a trace of that which is absent, a certainty forever deferred. Derrida's writing has been much compared to Nagarjuna, and he has also been critiqued for his failure to go far enough, remaining in a half-way house of textuality, while Buddhist thought points to a transformed way of experiencing the world in practice.[32]

Indeed, despite Heidegger's words about non-philosophy and the profundity of experience, his and other philosophies have largely ignored the most embodied and lived aspects of our experience. I was very taken with an observation by the great novelist Marilynne Robinson that if there is an emptiness prevalent in our age it is not because of the 'death of God' or an ebbing away of faith in the face of science, but more because of the 'exclusion of the felt life of the mind from the account of reality proposed'. She feels that this 'parascientific world view', along with the thought and art that reflects the influence of this view, 'has tended to forget the beauty and strangeness of the individual soul, that is, of the world as perceived in the course of a human life'.[33] In addition to the wonderful definition of 'soul', I think Robinson points to something important here – the gap between philosophy and experience.

A different response in the evasion of nihilism, and one that may provide some resolution of this gap, comes from the attempt to ground philosophy in embodiment undertaken in very different fashion first by Maurice Merleau-Ponty and later by the professor of linguistics George Lakoff and the philosopher Mark Johnson. Merleau-Ponty felt that the conventional view of experience of the body is a degeneration of lived experience into representation, and he wished us to see and question this familiar acceptance of it, then reconstruct it through attention. 'True philosophy consists in relearning to look at the world.'[34] He explored being-in-the-world from the perspective of the interface between the physiological and the psychological. This presents both mind and body and also subject and world as abstractions of presence, reinstating the embodied subject as one that is never distinct and separated, but always intentionally related to world. In this light the dynamic, lived relation of subject and world is revealed as pre-objective and pre-reflective. Unlike for Sartre, for whom this denoted exile, for Merleau-Ponty it is interconnection. His later work re-emphasizes this connection in terms of the 'chiasm', the intertwining of the visible and the invisible, the intersection of 'brute being' and 'flesh', the latter being a term that expresses our primordial bond with reality, or 'what is'. It is our openness to 'what is'. His writing expresses his attempt to encompass both the active and passive aspects of the lived body, which is both visible and seeing, and includes our relationship with the flesh of the world of which we participate and of which we are an articulation.

Over many years and through several texts, George Lakoff and Mark Johnson have defined an approach that they call 'Philosophy in the Flesh', an embodied realism that attempts to respond to the shifts in our contemporary understanding of embodiment, emotion and our relationship with our environment.[35] From a foundation of cognitive scientific understanding, they propose that reason can no longer be considered as disembodied and transcendent, but actually arises from the very nature of our brains, bodies and bodily experience. Their approach is also evolutionary, building on rather than attempting to ignore or transcend our animal nature, and it is not separated from emotion, being always and inevitably emotionally engaged. They acknowledge both that it is only the topmost levels of rational processes that are conscious, and that a sense of embodiment is centrally important to higher levels of consciousness. This last point arises from their earlier work, which demonstrated how language is embodied and metaphoric.

Language, they show, is formed from the imaginative and metaphoric extension of basic primary experiential statements. The categories and concepts we use to understand our world grow out of our bodily experience, and there can be no meaning without the structures and patterns that establish relationships. These organizing patterns and structures they term 'image schemata', which are recurring, dynamic patterns of our perceptual interactions with motor programmes. As a domain of subjective experience is co-activated regularly with a sensory-motor domain, permanent neural connections are established. The basic sensory-motor concepts are literal, but the primary metaphors that derive from our normal moving and perceiving in the world occur when a concept from this sensory-motor domain is imaginatively extended to apply to another domain of subjective experience. We can take concepts of spatial relations as an example of this. Spatial relations concepts make sense of space for us. We perceive an entity as *in*, *on*, *up*, *down*, *along from* and so on. Metaphorically we extend this embodied sensory spatial experience to the subjective valuing domain: good is *up*, bad is *down*, prices rise and fall, we aspire upwards and fall downwards both actually and morally.

Lakoff and Johnson have identified many other primary metaphor schemata, such as those of container and contained and source-path-goal. Even abstract concepts from love to morality may be traced back through multiple and complex metaphoric chains. Each primary metaphor is embodied in three ways: through our experience of the world, which pairs sensory-motor experience with subjective affective and evaluative experience; through the basic, neurally instantiated logic of perception and motor movement; and through neuroplasticity, the ongoing physical instantiation of frequent coactivation. Such processes take place largely below the level of consciousness.

Their philosophy also has a therapeutic intent. As with Wittgenstein's intention to show the fly out of the fly bottle, so by drawing attention to the power of metaphor in our speech, we may also appreciate how we normally fail to see this, taking language literally as we speak with the use of dead metaphors. This may help us to reuse language more consciously and more imaginatively, in a way that may enhance our experience. As an example of this Lakoff and Johnson point to the way so many of our descriptions of discussion and debate arise from metaphors of war. You win or lose an argument, arguments are shot down, weak points are attacked and so on. They suggest that we imagine a culture in which discussion is structured not by images of war, but rather of dance. There would then be no sense of attacking, gaining or losing ground, but rather a sense of performance, of being balanced or aesthetically pleasing. By such conscious inhabitation of not only language but also selves, we may rediscover the freedom we have, a freedom despite and within contingency and interdependence.

Again, this approach to philosophy upsets the traditional distinctions such as conscious–unconscious, body–mind and even individual–world. Our embodied experience provides the physical level for the metaphorical projection of imagination and speech, which informs the conceptual, social and historical dimensions of life, demonstrating the way we are meaningfully situated in the world through our bodily interactions, our linguistic traditions, cultural institutions and historical context. Understanding in this model is not a reflection on previous experience, but rather the very way we have – or, better still, *are* – that experience.

This shows again that boundaries are far more fluid than considered earlier. Nishitani saw all Western philosophy since Aristotle as being centred on a conception of substance as indicative of being, and a Buddhist commentator suggested, in the context of the work of Lakoff and Johnson, that they had omitted what is perhaps the most profound and pernicious of all metaphors: that of reality as substance.[36] It seems that this conception has been truly destabilized in recent times, and that echoes of emptiness and interconnection, hardly audible through many centuries, are drawing contemporary philosophy back to the Presocratic and Hellenistic philosophy of Greece and contemporary thought of India before the hegemony of substance and being, in an attempt to find an openness that is not nothing.

Emptiness is not always the term we find in these attempts. French philosophers, such as Maurice Blanchot and Roland Barthes especially, use the term 'neuter', or the neutral, to illustrate ideas that certainly cover some of the territory of emptiness. Blanchot describes the neutral as that which 'cannot be assigned to any genre whatsoever: the non-general, the non-generic, as well as the non-particular . . . the unknown'.[37] Barthes entitled a lecture course at the Collège de France *The Neutral*, defining it as 'the refusal to dogmatize'; that which 'outplays' or baffles the paradigm, defining paradigm as 'the opposition of two virtual terms, one of which must be chosen to produce meaning'; and 'the (philosophical) critique of 'it is'.[38] Back to the *ou mallon*. Indeed, many of the names and tropes cited by Barthes in his presentation of the neutral have appeared above; to name a few: Pyrrho, Tao, Zen, a guide to life, Christian mystics.

Most recently Hilary Lawson, self-described as a post-postmodern philosopher, in his story of closure has attempted to rewrite a non-ground without substance or presence. He describes how through closure, openness is divided into things.

> Without closure we would be lost in a sea of openness: a sea without character and without form. For in openness there is no colour, no sound, no distinguishing mark, no difference, no thing. Yet openness is not a thing, it is infinitely dense with possibility, but it is not differentiated.[39]

Each closure provides something not previously distinguished and at the same time is an obscuration of emptiness. Both sensation and language are forms of closure. Lawson also notes the transparency of the process: our closures are so familiar and self-reinforcing that the process of closure and 'the plasticity of openness' are obscured, with the consequence that the closures realized are taken as a description of the world. The overlap with emptiness surely occurs both in the presentation of openness and also in the impossibility of complete closure.

Lawson points to three areas of acknowledgement of this failure of closure and the search for openness: experiential, artistic and religious. First, he describes the desire to approach the edge of closure in search of the unknown, when we realize that our language fails to measure up to our experience. This, I believe, resonates with ideas of the Sublime. Second, there is the more self-aware attempt of the artist to acknowledge the failure of closure and the avoidance of any attempt at complete closure. Third, there is the domain of religion and philosophy in the attempt to name, or at least point to, the unnameable.

In writing this Lawson was not familiar with the work of Nagarjuna or any Eastern philosophers. He understands, however, like them, that the

> search for openness and the search for closure are . . . mirror images of each other. Both are sought and both are unattainable, and for the same reason. They are the product of the process of closure, and the process of closure involves the play of both closure and openness.

One voice recently has opposed the trend of relativism and correlationism that posits that everything meaningful is constrained by the limits of human understanding. In order to provide an answer to the problem of the 'ancestral', reality prior to the emergence of human experience, consciousness and language, the French philosopher Quentin Meillassoux has called for the return of necessity and an absolute. Paradoxically the absolute necessity for which he argues is that of contingency.

Closure and openness, necessity and contingency. Emptiness and form, form and emptiness.[40]

# SIX

# Scientific Indeterminism

Reality is under constant review.

Paul Broks, *Into the Silent Land*

It does not take a scientist to see that the reality of the world as demonstrated by today's science appears to be very different from the way we have traditionally considered it to be. While Lucretius in the first century BC wrote of matter and void and stated that 'everything is riddled with emptiness', believing that 'if there were no emptiness, nothing could move', throughout the centuries science has been more concerned with matter than with emptiness.[1] Yet as twentieth-century scientists were investigating matter and form, they increasingly discovered indeterminacy and emptiness. Einstein's famous equation $e = mc^2$ signposted the path into uncertainty, a path already marked by inevitable randomness and decline in a world governed by entropy. As a result, much of the most contemporary philosophy today is engaging with the dialogue with science.

Einstein's initial discovery of the Theory of Relativity has over time led on to theories of indeterminacy, quantum theory, string theory, chaos theory, anti-matter, black holes, quarks and the elusive Higgs Boson, all of which have only widened this divide between the view of science and our common, everyday understanding of the world. We live in a world that is in actuality very different from the way we perceive it. Writing of the recently (possibly) discovered Higgs boson particle, a

*Newsweek* article suggests that it validates 'an unprecedented revolution in our understanding of fundamental physics'. The discovery of this particle predicts an invisible field pervading space, and suggests that matter and the forces that control our existence arise from their interaction with empty space, so, the writer continues, confirming 'the notion that seemingly empty space may contain the seeds of our existence'.[2]

Perhaps a good illustration of this, which is also an illustration of the similar relationship between emptiness and interdependence – the dependent origination of Early Buddhist thought – is that of scientists sitting at a table, which they know is full of waves and particles in space at the quantum level, yet they trust its solidity as a surface on which to write. As with philosophy, it is these relatively recent changes within science itself that have resonated with emptiness. As reality appears evermore strange to our everyday view, philosophy and science are perhaps becoming close. Philosophers such as Evan Thompson, Thomas Metzinger, Alva Noë and Owen Flanagan weave understanding of the history of Western thought alongside the daily changing discoveries of neuroscience, realizing that today to separate our knowledge from understanding the process of gaining that knowledge is to present but a partial picture.

## NEW PARADIGMS

The publication of Einstein's paper on the Special Theory of Relativity in 1905 is thought to have marked the beginning of post-classical physics. This was reinforced a little later with the development of quantum theory. In the view of classical physics, the world was composed of discrete particles with defined properties interacting in accordance with deterministic laws. By the beginning of the twentieth century it was clear that such explanations failed to account for some phenomena.

The Newtonian universe presented an unchangeable and immovable, three-dimensional space. Change was thought to occur in the dimension of time, which was also considered absolute, unconnected with the material world, and flowed smoothly from past, through present, into future. Within this space and time, material particles moved according to natural forces. It was in response to the need to find a common framework for this mechanical view and that of electrodynamics that Einstein devised the Special Theory of Relativity – the start of an upheaval of our understanding of the world and of a movement from certainty and quantifiability to indeterminacy and complexity, and a new paradigm for physics. According to relativity theory, space is not three-dimensional, nor is time a separate entity. Space and time are intimately connected in a four-dimensional space–time continuum. The even and universal flow of time disappears, too: different observers will order events differently in time if they move at different speeds in relation to the events observed. Thus space and time lose their absolute characteristics.

Along with this Einstein discovered that matter is a form of energy. This resulted in the famous equation $e = mc^2$, where c is the constant, the speed of light.[3] In 1915 Einstein proposed his General Theory of Relativity, extending the framework of the Special Theory to include gravity. The force of gravity has the effect of curving space and time. Science from the times of Democritus and of Newton had dealt with matter and empty space – the full and the empty. From the time of general relativity, the two can no longer be separated; matter and space are seen to be inseparable and interdependent parts of a whole. The old, mechanistic view of classical physics, of solid objects moving in empty space, still holds good in the region of our daily experience, in the zone of middle dimensions, which may explain why for most of us this knowledge, which has been around now for nearly a century, still fails to be recognized in our daily understanding. Beyond this, however, in the almost un-imaginable spaces of cosmology and astrophysics, empty space has lost its meaning; it is not devoid of anything but pulsing with qualities and potentialities. This is reflected in the title of a recent book, *The 4% Universe: Dark Matter, Dark Energy, and the Race to Discover the Rest of Reality* by Richard Panek. A review of this book neatly encapsulated the extent of the unknown and explained the title, stating that the major component of the universe, some 73 per cent of its substance is:

> 'dark energy' – so called because no one has the faintest idea what it really is. Next, with 23%, comes 'dark matter' – so called partly because you can't see it with a telescope, even though it seems it must be there to hold the struc-tures of the universe together, but also because there are only hints and suppositions as to what this mysterious substance might be. The remaining 4% is the stuff of you and me, and of the 'next Newton', who Panek suggests will be required to unite the physics of the very small with the physics of the very big and shed some light on all this darkness.[4]

At the other end of the scale, particle physics has shattered the concept of solid objects. Quantum physics further demolished our commonsense view of the world. The subatomic units of matter appear as very abstract entities with dual aspects, appearing sometimes as waves, sometimes as particles, accord-ing to how we look at them. Features of quantum theory are not familiar in daily experience: quantization, the duality of wave and particle, complementarity, uncertainty and indeter-minacy, probabilistic prediction, the problem of quantum measurement and non-locality. Whereas according to classical physics there are waves and particles, in quantum theory some particles, such as electrons, may behave like waves under certain circumstances, while waves may also demonstrate particle properties. An electron, for example, cannot in itself be defined as either a wave or a particle; it can only be said to have wave or particle nature in relation to a given situation. That something may never act as particle and wave at the same moment is an example of the notion of complementarity. There is a further conundrum; it is impossible to accurately determine the position and momentum of a particle simultaneously. The laws of atomic physics are expressed in terms of probabilities, not certainties; events do not occur with certainty in definite places and times, but rather show a tendency to exist or a tendency to occur. This is an example of Heisenberg's uncertainty principle, often explained by the fact that when we measure anything at the quantum level the experimenter inevitably disturbs the experiment. However, more than this:

> it is not that the electron really has a definite position and momentum but we cannot know what they are; rather, the electron's position and moment have a certain irreducible 'fuzziness.'[5]

Thus, while classical physics is deterministic, quantum theory must be described as probabilistic, as demonstrated in the often-cited thought experiment of Schrödinger's cat, which illustrates the difficulty of holding the view of quantum reality and that of classical physics simultaneously, in the question of when and whether the cat is dead or alive.

Emptiness is thus very much at the heart of the new physics, whether in great or minuscule scale. A recent television programme on the subject of gravity attempted to explain an atom, which in its very name means 'indivisible' (from the Greek, *atomos*), but which we now know is indeed divisible into many subatomic particles. It demonstrated how all of the atom's mass is in its nucleus, which is tiny and surrounded by empty space in which travels a cloud of electrons like specks of dust. Matter, thus, is almost entirely empty. Since everything in the universe is made up of atoms, and atoms are over 99.9 per cent empty space, 'most of the universe is empty', explained the presenter.[6]

In an interesting reversal of influence, a Buddhist writer in a commentary to the Heart Sutra, whose most famous opening line states that 'Form is Emptiness, Emptiness is Form', suggests that our

> current understanding of Buddhist meditative experiences has also been greatly facilitated by the findings of quantum physics with regard to the nature of ultimate reality; these findings have added a new dimension to our efforts to understand the meaning of shunyata.[7]

In 1930 another theory provided a nail in the coffin of any theory of singularity and definability. In Königsberg, the city in which Kant was born, Kurt Gödel first presented his incompleteness theorum, which postulated that it is impossible for any consistent formal system to exist without including propositions that, within the limits of that system, are undecidable. To support such systems there is always the necessity for a rule or proposition that is outside the system. This was seen to challenge the foundations of mathematics. An emptiness, an essential unfindability, at the heart of discourse.

While it is perhaps in philosophical terms a category error to extrapolate from the science of the immense or the very small to the dimensions and concerns of everyday human life, I hope I have described enough to demonstrate that throughout the new scientific paradigm, certain themes recur – themes that trouble previous certainties, and that we are meeting time and again in these pages in different disciplines. Classical science dealt with substance, with fundamental building blocks from which, according to laws of interaction, greater wholes would be built up. In the new paradigm the relationship between part and whole is changed; rather than a mechanical universe built up of substantial blocks, we are presented with a network of relationships in which a part is merely a pattern that has some stability. Thus there is a movement from thinking in terms of structure to that of dynamic process. This requires a shift from a language of foundation and construction to one of networks and relationships. The recognition embodied in the Theory of Special Relativity, that mass is a form of energy, changed the reference from particles of material stuff to patterns of energy, from architectural metaphors to dynamic ones, from essence to process.

Another major shift concerns the position of the researcher. The objectivity of scientific description is no longer absolutely viable and understanding of the process of knowledge has to be included in the description of the process. This leads to a more participatory understanding. The acknowledgement of interconnectivity leads also to a shift from the search for an absolute truth to one of recognizing that any truth may be approximate and partial.

These relatively recent theories and discoveries in the fields of physics and mathematics have, as we see, moved away from the idea of a mechanistic universe and linear models towards an understanding of wider process and interdependence. Similar change has occurred in other branches of science. The theory of living, self-organizing systems, arising from the work of Ilya Prigogine, Gregory Bateson, Humberto Maturana and Francisco Varela, has been applied to individual living organisms, social systems and ecosystems. This has given rise to systems theory, chaos theory, complexity theory, the Gaia hypothesis and holistic science. Such theories show the same tendencies and shifts as those outlined above. Where classical science explained closed systems and the physical behaviours of mechanical objects, this contemporary science has arisen from attempts to understand dynamic, open and complex systems such as weather, ecosystems and consciousness.

Such a radical reframing of reality comes largely from a different vision of causality, wherein a consequence is seen to arise from a network of multiple causes rather than from a direct, single cause. Complex systems such as brain function develop 'emergent' properties generated by interactions within the system as a whole, rather than by the actions of any single part. These emergent properties are more than the sum of their parts. At high levels of complexity they also demonstrate their own causal power, producing top-down changes to lower levels of the system. Thus we find two-way causation, both bottom-up and top-down. This notion of non-linear or emergent dynamics replacing earlier mechanistic models has stimulated new approaches to old problems, such as the relations between the biological and the mental, the physical and the experiential, the personal and the social. Non-linear dynamic network models now replace linear, hierarchical ones; a concern for context and complexity supplants attention to isolated events and reductive models, and the emphasis is on process rather than product.

One of the first theories to emerge from these new views was that of autopoesis, or self-creation, first described by Humberto Maturana and Francisco Varela. It describes the process of renewal whereby an organism, from cell to society, may create and recreate itself by regulating its own internal environment within limits conducive to its continuing existence. It does this by constantly remaking and rearranging the components of the complex networks operating inside its semi-permeable boundary. It is an illustration of the dynamic interchange between emptiness of essence and interdependence, and how, understanding the emptiness of essence at the heart of phenomena, we may also understand our participation in ever-changing process.

Moving up the scale from the individual to the whole context, ecology is the child of contemporary science that reflects many of these tropes. According to Arne Næss, the founder of deep ecology (and incidentally a self-admitted Pyrrhonian Sceptic), ecology suggests 'a relational total field image [in which] organisms [are] knots in a biospherical net of intrinsic relations'.[8] Discussing this, J. Baird Callicott describes how at the philosophical level of discourse, ecology requires a shift from talking of reality in terms of atomism to that of field theory, and of events rather than objects. In the concept of nature implied by this, energy and relationships become fundamental realities more than discrete objects. Such an attitude is inevitably holistic and it becomes impossible to fully consider an object in isolation from its context. Such holism importantly is an immanent one, a unity in diversity or diverse unity that in no way points to any transcendence beyond appearances. Nature is just and sufficiently a differentiated whole.

Ecology is pre-eminently the science of pattern, context, interdependence and the understanding of networks, and could be described as the living face of dependent or conditioned arising, the form side or counterpart of emptiness. As Gary Snyder described it, it is 'a valuable shorthand term for complexity in motion'.[9]

All of this sounds familiar from the perspective of emptiness and dependent origination, a fact noted by several observers. As stated by the Dalai Lama:

Their [events and facts'] existence and reality can make sense only within the context of interrelationships and interconnectedness. Insofar as certain experiments in quantum physics point towards an understanding of the nonsubstantiality of material things, then perhaps there is a meaningful parallel with the Buddhist concept of emptiness.[10]

Phenomena do not appear to exist independently and intrinsically; their attributes are relational. We have here a picture of a participatory universe, one that lies at the foundation of the approach of holistic science, for as the Dalai Lama noted, 'Emptiness has a direct relevance to the person's worldview and relationship to the world.'[11]

It might be interesting at this stage to note that while trends in contemporary science – of process, contingency and inter-relationship – might appear to be leading us towards ways of thinking closer to those of the East and away from the dualistic models of earlier Western thought, without those models, of substance and reason, there would have been no science as we know it. The Western divisions of material and mind, faith and reason, heaven and world, allowed for the explorations of nature as 'other' in a manner that the more participatory under-standing that we have seen in traditional Chinese thought failed to encourage.

Moreover, the echoes of emptiness we find in contemporary Western science and arts practice have a vital distinction from the worked-out philosophy of emptiness expressed in Buddhist and Taoist thought. Their source is perhaps similar: the experi-ence of the individual, namely in the latter case the Buddha, and in the former case the many scientists and artists who have dis-covered it as a feature of their own physical and existential reality. However, the intention of teaching or expressing it is different. In Buddhism it is soteriological; understanding of emptiness and interdependence will lead to liberation from ignorance and from emotional binding. In Western contexts, it is usually descriptive rather than prescriptive. While descriptions of emptiness are common in contemporary science, the implications of this new knowledge for ethics, education, child rearing and the normal business of daily life are as yet seldom explored in depth. Even in the field of the mind sciences, where self is seen as normatively empty and constructed, the implications of this for lived experience are rarely investigated, although the repercussions of the burgeoning knowledge of brain work and brain development are profound for the fields of education and developmental studies.

### NOT-SELF IN THE FIELD OF THE MIND SCIENCES

We are a shape the wind makes in these leaves as it passes through.
Jack Gilbert, *Music is in the Piano Only When it is Played*

Minds emerge from process and interaction, not substance. In a sense, we inhabit the spaces between things. We subsist in emptiness. A beautiful, liberating thought and nothing to be afraid of.
Paul Broks, *Into the Silent Land*

Today in the field of the mind sciences we find a deconstruction of our normally understood definitions of self that bear comparison with the teachings of Early Buddhism. Self appears to science today as a construction, a process of composition free from attribution as an independent thing, substance or governor. I use the term mind sciences to denote the whole field that encompasses the work of the once separate domains of psychology, psychotherapy, cognitive science and now the ever-proliferating disciplines of consciousness studies, and cognitive, emotional and even contemplative neuroscience. In this new interdisciplinary field we find the collaboration of all of the above, and also of philosophers of mind and ethics, linguists and psychiatrists, among others – all of which reflects the distribution of the contemporary concept of self. The mind sciences have for many years undertaken the analysis, deconstruction and description of the processes that form what we still, ruled by language and folk psychology, term and consider 'the self'. Today it is not so much divided as fragmented.

There are many models describing the development and construction of a sense of self. One of the most cited is that of the neuroscientist Antonio Damasio, which posits a proto-self, a core-self and an autobiographical self. Almost all models begin with basic bodily awareness, followed by some method of representation of one's physical state; a movement from self-monitoring to self-awareness that leads to the imposition of 'self' on to system. Once this is symbolized within language, it is reinforced and reified by the social structures and value systems of the cultural sphere. Such models follow a path from some form of immediate self-awareness to some form of narrative self, a coherent concept that stretches back into the past and forwards into the future. All agree that there is no such *thing* as a self. As described by a neuropsychologist:

> From a neuroscience perspective we are all divided and discontinuous. The mental processes underlying our sense of self – feelings, thought, memories – are scattered through different zones of the brain. There is no special point of convergence. No cockpit of the soul. No soul-pilot. They come together as a work of fiction. A human being is a story-telling machine. The self is a story.[12]

Similarly, the self has been described by Daniel Dennett as 'the centre of narrative gravity', and the function of selfing allotted to the 'left brain interpreter' by Michael Gazzaniga.[13] The philosopher Charles Taylor, citing the work of Merleau-Ponty, Heidegger, Wittgenstein and Michael Polanyi, has noted that much of the most insightful philosophy of the twentieth century has refuted the picture of the disengaged subject.[14] William James in the early days of the discipline of psychology was one of the first to challenge the traditional view of the self as some kind of independent homunculus in the mind. At the beginning of the twentieth century he described it as distributed between the material self, which included body, family and possession; the social self, the recognition we receive from others; and the spiritual self, the inner or psychic dispositions and the pure ego, concluding that 'the self of selves when carefully examined, is found to consist mainly of the collection of these peculiar motions in the head, or between the head and the throat'.[15]

Since James, there has been profound and widespread expansion of our knowledge of the development of the self, most of which has occurred in the relatively recent past. Interestingly, there was a long period in which his writings, grounded in phenomenal and subjective understanding, were ignored. During this time psychology, which one might imagine to be the study of human experience, paradoxically refused to consider subjective conscious experience at all, and considered only visible and quantifiable behaviours as appropriate objects of research. During these years concern with lived experience was taken up by psychotherapies of many different persuasions. However, since the last decades of the twentieth century the many disciplines that together form the field of the mind sciences have taken enormous strides towards understanding consciousness. Today we are beginning to understand something of how our minds work, how they develop in childhood and beyond, and thus how we may best encourage their development and effect repair when necessary.

This new knowledge challenges much of our earlier beliefs. It seems that much of our fundamental thinking about our selves is false: for example, our minds and bodies are seen to be inseparable, and our reason and emotion thoroughly interconnected. As described by the anthropologist Clifford Geertz, bringing these points together:

Our brains are not in a vat, but in our bodies. Our minds are not in our bodies, but in the world. And as for the world, it is not in our brains, our bodies or in our minds: they are, along with gods, verbs, rock and politics, in it.[16]

Moreover, much of what we have considered to be most human about ourselves is seen to happen quite happily below the level of consciousness. Nor can individuals usefully be considered in isolation from their environment, be it physical, social or cultural. Most exciting, perhaps, is the acknowledgement of neuroplasticity, the process whereby the brain continually changes in response to our experience, both through forming new connections between neurons and through the generation of new neurons. This applies not only to experience of external activity, but also to that of purely internal, mental activity. In the often-repeated words applied to the work of the early Canadian psychologist Donald Hebb: 'neurons that fire together, wire together'. Neuroplasticity enables the ability to significantly change both the structures and patterns of activity, not only in childhood but also throughout our lives.

While much of what we consider most nearly to be our selves actually occurs below the level of consciousness and control, there are actions that we can take, practices we can cultivate to assist desired change. Constant re-engagement and thus strengthening of the neurological pathways leading to certain feelings and actions can influence our development for better or worse. Indeed, to some extent at least, in the words of one of the oldest Buddhist texts, 'with our minds we make our world', in a constant feedback process.

Between the time of James and neuropsychology, within the discipline of psychology and the practice of psychotherapy, the self has been analysed, divided and distributed in many different ways. From Freud's division into conscious, preconscious and unconscious, superego, ego and id, through the object relations school's understanding of the infant's developmental dependence on interaction with others, we can say that different approaches, analytic, humanistic and transpersonal, have seen the image of the self as covering an ever-expanding area: intra-, inter- and trans-personal. In 1991 a somewhat tongue-in-cheek article on the subject of models of self referred to cognitive self, conceptual self, contextualized self, core self, dialogic self, ecological self, embodied self, emergent self, empirical self, existential self, extended self, fictional self, full-grown self, interpersonal self, material self, narrative self, philosophical self, private self, representational self, rock-bottom essential self, semiotic self, social self, transparent self and verbal self.[17] The list must by now be far longer. Such a long list of different aspects of the self surely demonstrates that it is process rather than substance, that it lacks individual essence and is thoroughly constructed, compounded and ever-changeful – in short, empty.

Jacques Lacan is an important figure in whose writings and practice in psychoanalysis we may find echoes of emptiness. Lacan saw the development of the individual in terms of three stages, or orders, a process that he saw as occurring through the symbolic and linguistic rather than the biological. The first stage, which he calls the Imaginary, is the condition of being, before entry into language, in which there is no clear division between subject and object, and which involves a pre-symbolic identification with, usually, the mother. The child then passes into the Symbolic stage, based on language, culture and social exchange. This, according to Lacan, is the realm of conventional meaning. The turning point between the two is what he termed the mirror stage, a period at which infants, still without mastery of their own body, see their image in a mirror as coherent and selfgoverning. At this moment an infant sees the distinction of self and other, and this is the moment in which subjectivity is born. Subjectivity is the term used by Derrida and Lacan to signify the way in which human identity is determined by other forces, linguistic, cultural and social. The ego is born from this identification with an image. This ego, however, is at heart what Lacan calls a *méconnaissance*, a mis- or false recognition; it is an alienating identification, due to the misalliance between the image of coherence and the actual lack of it. This model demonstrates the ongoing tension between the empty nature of our selves and of everything, and our continual efforts, at many levels of mind and body, to reify and make solid what is fleeting and changeable, which is the cause of much anxiety.

The human search for imaginary wholeness and unity is a futile project, according to Lacan, as the ego seeks endless substitutes for the loss of what it desires: the third realm, the Real. The Real, however, stands for the impossibility or void at the heart of the Symbolic, which is forever unattainable. At the heart of the Real (not reality, but that which is neither imaginary nor symbolic) is emptiness, undefinability. It may be gestured towards but never grasped, is impossible and unattainable. Thus the Lacanian project is a study of loss or lack. Understanding the illusion, Lacan's practice was to allow the individual to come to terms with their alienated identity and understand that their desire for wholeness is illusory desire for something that does not exist. Understanding this, they may lose both illusion and sense of lack, and they may get on with their lives.

One of the most recent and most profound descriptions of the process of self- and world creation comes from the philosopher of mind Thomas Metzinger, in an exploration of consciousness from the perspective of both philosophy and science. He describes (and here I simplify, I hope not unforgivably) the formation of what he terms a phenomenal self-model that shows the way information is integrated and unified in the mind by the mapping of physical process back on to itself, so it becomes its own context. He explains how this is most probably achieved through a synchrony of neural responses that binds features together. Consciousness thus 'makes the world present for you by creating a new space in your mind – the space of temporal internality. Everything is *in the Now*.'[18] This creates, he says, a tunnel of presence that he calls the Ego Tunnel: 'The Ego Tunnel is just the opposite of the God's-eye view of the world. It has a Now, a Here – and a Me, *being there now*.'[19]

So far so good – what, however, may not be so good, is that this tunnel is transparent. We cannot be aware *of* it, we can only experience *through* it. What we experience is thus a representation that we imagine is reality. It is actually empty of the independence and authority with which we normally credit it.

Why is all this deconstruction of the self important? A self is obviously useful as a means of identification and a centre of gravity for ongoing action. We need to feel ourselves the same self on waking as the one we left as we fell asleep: others need to be able to recognize us day by day. However, it becomes unhelpful when we hold it too tightly, and see it too literally as an isolated object rather than as a representation or a process. This harms us individually by denying flexibility and resilience amid inevitably changing circumstances, and also socially by encouraging selfishness and self-centred understanding. We mistake the process of selfing for a finished self-image. Again, what is necessary is a middle way – between loss of all conception of self, and grasping it as a permanent, independent and unchanging structure.

It is an exciting time in the mind sciences. For the first time what has been experientially and philosophically described from a psychological perspective is being translated into the scientific language of visible brain states. Developmental psychologies, particularly John Bowlby's theories of attachment, have now been reinterpreted in terms of neurology and chemistry.[20] Neuroplasticity, showing that development is a two-way process, our brains affecting how we experience the world and that experience changing the conformation of our brains, has important implications for health, education and therapy. If we are creatures of habit, we may select the habits that will encourage mental and subsequent physical health. We can now see and know how various emotions, stress and fear affect the brain and body. Those who are at the forefront of affective neuroscience, such as Richard Davidson and the neuropsychologist Rick Hanson, have written with particular intention to help us enhance our well-being and resilience, by consciously encouraging supportive practices.[21]

We can strengthen positive feelings by imagining the scenarios in which we experience love and affirmation. By cultivation of attention we can strengthen the neuronal connections that enhance feelings of well-being. By paying attention to attention itself we can watch how our minds work: how the emotions we feel and the stories we tell ourselves quickly colour the events and the facts of any situation, adding value and embellishment that we then take to be indivisible from the bare experience. Through careful, non-judgemental attention, we can understand that the self is not solid and permanent, but is constructed from these emotions and predispositions that impinge on our experience moment by moment. We can learn to discriminate between the acting process of self and self-image and understand that our selves are complex and interdependent, always changeable processes that engage and involve body, mind and the world of things and interpersonal relations that surround us. Separating out the different strands, daring to move beyond certainty and fixed identity, we may free ourselves from defensiveness and fear that ever-changing circumstances are attacking a 'thing' called 'myself', learn how to be more comfortable with unknowing and open up space for choice, rather than rushing into unconsidered, fearful and defensive reaction. Slowly, thus, we first identify our habitual patterns in order to initiate new ones more conducive to equanimity and well-being. These new patterns will then be instantiated into our brains in a virtuous cycle.

From the perspective of a philosophy of emptiness, particularly interesting and unignorable are the echoes of Buddhism's first psychology – the constructed nature of self and phenomena, and the power of emotions, thoughts and dispositions in our understanding of them. Such resonance with the Buddhist teachings explored earlier may arise because the Buddha's teachings were based on experience and on the subjective analysis of mind with the intention to end suffering. Practices of attention, mindfulness and meditation are undertaken with the intention of lessening natural ignorance and evading emotional dysfunction, exposing the Ego Tunnel by bringing attention to the very way the mind works. This is a good model for psychotherapy even today. All change begins in awareness. Understanding the emptiness of a reified self-image in contrast to the real and necessary but ever-changing process or project of selfing, is the very lifeblood of psychotherapeutic work. When we identify with an unchanging identity that has been created by our experience and the labels given to us by others, we are trapped in a straitjacket that may prove constricting when our experience changes. If we can see our selves as flexible, impermanent and changeable, we may be much more resilient in the face of ever-changing life. As the child said to the parent: 'If I had a permanent self, how could I ever grow up?'

For these reasons, the dialogue between psychology and Buddhist teachings has been the longest and most fruitful of any between Buddhism and other Western disciplines.[22] There is a much-repeated story of a visiting Buddhist monk attending one of William James's seminars; James is said to have suggested that the monk's psychology would be the psychology of the future. This has not exactly come to pass that clearly, but there is no doubt that the dialogue is strong, and getting stronger, particularly in the recent neuroscientific research into practices of mindfulness, abstracted from any religious context, for the enhancement of well-being and the relief of chronic pain, and of stress and depression.

A series of meetings occurring almost annually over twenty years between the Dalai Lama and Western scientists has now resulted in annual summer schools offering meditative trainings for scientists, and also in many research projects using Western scientific techniques to explore Eastern subjective practices in order that first-person subjective mind training and third-person objective research procedures may come together in experienced practice.[23] As encouraged by the Dalai Lama, scientific research into brain function has also concerned itself with positive emotions such as compassion and well-being, rather than pathology as was previously the inclination.

Such experiments are important, for if, as Buddhist teachings state, misunderstanding of the self and of phenomena is perpetuated by the pride of identifying with ourselves, by possessiveness and by erroneous views of self, we could say that Western psychology has come to terms with erroneous views in theory. However, it has failed to shift the everyday experiential understanding of the self in practice along with our identification with self-image, the emotions with which we hold on to it and the possessive manner (in terms both psychological and consumerist) with which we attempt to support it.

In 2008 the columnist David Brooks wrote a piece for the *New York Times* entitled 'The Neural Buddhists'.[24] In it he suggested that the atheism debate between scientific materialists and believers would become a mere sideshow, and that the cognitive revolution would not end up undermining faith in God, but rather faith in the Bible. He cited recent neurological research as revealing, for example, the importance of interpersonal relations, universal moral intuitions and the existence of transcendent (or non-self-centred) states. Such research, he felt, would not give rise to militant atheism, but rather what he suggested 'you might call neural Buddhism'. He defines the pillars of such understanding in this way:

> First, the self is not a fixed entity but a dynamic process of relationships. Second, underneath the patina of different religions, people around the world have common moral intuitions. Third, people are equipped to experience the sacred, to have moments of elevated experience when they transcend boundaries and overflow with love. Fourth, God can best be conceived as the nature one experiences at those moments, the unknowable total of all there is.

Awareness practices, philosophy and the mind sciences are coming together, uniting Western, scientific, third-person, objective research methods and ancient, subjective, first-person practices of mind exploration and awareness training to explore consciousness in projects involving many different disciplines, such as neurophenomenology. It is as common now for philosophers such as Metzinger, Owen Flanagan and Evan Thompson to write about consciousness with full understanding of brain science, as it is for scientists such as Antonio Damasio to write of Spinoza, and for all of the above to meet with the Dalai Lama and long-term practitioners of meditation. Also, these new discoveries about our minds have serious implications in practice for how we may best live. Mindfulness training is now available within the UK National Health Service. Mindfulness, when brought together with cognitive behavioural therapy, is one of the most current of contemporary psychotherapies, being espoused by medical authorities in both the United States and Europe. Mindfulness training is now to be found far beyond its original medical application in the treatment of chronic pain, stress and depression, in the fields of education, business and sport.

This new knowledge, as Metzinger points out, has important ethical and educational implications. The increasing knowledge of consciousness also leads to an increasing ability to manipulate and alter it, leading to serious questions as to what is desirable and what is undesirable. The first question, he suggests, must be what a 'good' state of consciousness would be. How and who shall decide? What should be taught? What should be forbidden?

He also points to a related problem in the management of our attention. He considers that the ability to attend is a naturally evolved feature of the human brain, and sees consciousness as the space of attentional agency, so that 'the experience of controlling and sustaining your focus of attention is one of the deeper layers of phenomenal selfhood.'[25] Metzinger sees the media environment of contemporary culture as 'not only an organized attack on the space of consciousness *per se* but a mild form of depersonalization', and proposes the introduction of meditation instruction in high schools so that young people may be made aware of the limited nature of their attentional capacity, and the need to learn techniques to enhance mindfulness and the sustaining of attention. Such training should, of course, be free of any religious trappings and might, he suggests, be presented as part of physical education classes, thus underlining the inseparability of mental and physical potential. This echoes William James's words from over 100 years earlier:

> The faculty of voluntarily bringing back a wandering attention over and over again is the very root of judgement, character and will. No one is *compos sui* if he have it not. An education which should improve this faculty would be *the* education *par excellence*. But it is easier to define this ideal than to give practical directions for bringing it about.[26]

The psychiatrist, philosopher and writer Iain McGilchrist, like Metzinger, is disturbed by our current paradigm of consciousness. He interprets the problem as a lack of balance in the value placed on the function of the two hemispheres of the brain. He too sees attention as at the heart of the matter:

> Things change according to the stance we adopt towards them, the type of attention we pay to them, the disposition we hold in relation to them ... The kind of attention we pay actually alters the world: we are, literally, partners in creation.[27]

McGilchrist argues that the distinction and asymmetry between the hemispheres of the brain lies not in what they do, but in how they do it. Attention also is a relationship, a 'howness' rather than a 'whatness', not itself an object of consciousness. We pay attention in different ways, and thus experience and create our world differently according to the primacy of one or other hemisphere. He suggests that the right hemisphere takes the broader view, is open to whatever exists apart from ourselves and is responsible for all types of attention except focused attention. The left hemisphere is dominant for highly focused attention, apprehending what the right hemisphere has brought into being for itself as a representation. The left hemisphere is the hemisphere of utility, of abstraction concerned with parts, while the right hemisphere sees the whole, sees interconnection and context. Due to its openness to interconnection, the right hemisphere is also the locus of empathic identification.

Such extrapolation from a massive and well-documented and well-referenced book inevitably leads to over-generalization; the picture in detail is inescapably more complicated. Empathy, for example, is also accomplished by theory of mind activities, which involve left-hemisphere activity concerned with interior language. Also, this lateralization is reversed for about half of all left-handed people. However, I think the most important point in McGilchrist's argument is that he is concerned not with the function of the two hemispheres, but with the manner of their functioning, the *how* and not the *what*.

McGilchrist is concerned that our current culture is under the hegemony of the left-hemispheric approach, which creates a sort of self-reflexive virtual world, a fragmented and decontextualized world that results in unwarranted optimism mixed with feelings of emptiness as lack. Interestingly, his descriptions of the two hemispheres have considerable overlap with the egocentric and allocentric outlooks that James Austin writes about, noted in chapter One. The right hemisphere

> pays attention to the Other, whatever it is that exists apart from ourselves with which it sees itself in profound relation . . . By contrast, the left hemisphere pays attention to the virtual world that it has created, which is self-consistent, but self-contained, ultimately disconnected from the Other, making it powerful, but ultimately only able to operate on, and to know, itself.[28]

Since it can know only itself, interpreting the world from this perspective the left hemisphere negates the reality of the right hemisphere in a manner equivalent to that in which Metzinger's Ego Tunnel prevents real knowledge of the selfing process. Similarly, the results are deleterious. Science, being a predominantly left-hemisphere activity, has such a position of power in Western culture that the reality of the right hemisphere is being increasingly ignored, and thus our creation of our world is unbalanced. The world of the left hemisphere is explicit, localized and represented; that of the right contextual, embedded and implicit. According to McGilchrist the right hemisphere should be the master and the left the emissary, since 'The right hemisphere is the primary mediator of experience, from which the conceptualized, re-presented world of the left hemisphere derives, and on which it depends.'[29]

The currency of the right hemisphere is encounter; that of the left, information – an echo of Heidegger's concern with 'framing'. McGilchrist believes that currently the master has become the emissary. I have quoted from this book as, apart from its own richness of research, I was taken with the resonance of McGilchrist's descriptions of the right hemisphere and his explorations around it with my own examination of expressions of emptiness and the manner in which both point to the value of practices of attention. McGilchrist suggests that 'Perhaps indeed everything that exists does so only in relationships, like mathematics or music: there are aspects of quantum physics that would support such a view.'[30] Perhaps, then, the emptiness of self is not such a strange idea.

# SEVEN

# Artistic Emptiness

Ultimately, one's unbound curiosity about these empty zones
about these objectless vistas, is what art seems to be all about.

Joseph Brodsky, *New Life*

In a world addicted to consumption and power, art celebrates
emptiness and surrender. In a world accelerating to greater
and greater speed, art reminds us of the timeless.

J. L. Adams, *Winter Music*

Why emptiness? Without emptiness, without space, there is no
room for imagination, for creativity, for things to be other than
they are. Ursula K. Le Guin, author of extraordinary writings,
particularly in the field of science fiction, in which she has
invented truly 'other' worlds, has noted that 'The exercise of
the imagination is dangerous to those who profit from the ways
things are because it has the power to show that the way things
are is not permanent, not universal, not necessary.'[1]

In the spacious field of the arts, artists are, as Joseph Brodsky
expressed in the quotation above, those who have the most
curiosity, courage and commitment to go into the empty zones.
It is from here that in the last centuries they have brought back
echoes of emptiness to challenge a culture that is increasingly
desperate about filling every moment, every space and every
silence to evade an emptiness that is seen only as lack. Iain
McGilchrist has expressed his concern about what he sees as the

ever-increasing hegemony of left-hemisphere ways of paying attention to the world. Imagination, a process of predominately right-hemispheric processes, he sees as critical to attempts to redress this imbalance. This would ally the right-hemisphere, holistic presentation of the world to left-hemisphere analysis and representation, enabling a dialectical balance rather than simple attachment to the decontextualized and unimaginative tunnel of the left, where things are seen to be both more certain and less fruitful than they may be. The arts of the past century or so, I believe, reflect this trend, both in the hegemony of left-hemispheric bias towards an emptiness of lack, and also in the many voices that struggle to reconnect with a wider perspective, an emptiness of potential, unknowing and imagination. It is these latter especially that I shall be seeking to name here.

Themes seen in philosophy and the sciences play out in all the fields of the arts. In form, we see the breaking down of barriers between genres and between artist and audience, and movements towards process, rather than product and substance. In content, we find the tropes of loss and lack weaving echoes of emptiness into all discourse: in the visual arts the loss of the object, in music the breakdown of traditional rules and structures and of authorial authority, and in literature the collapse of the integrity of the narrator. And yet, playing with such lack, much of the work produced shows, even embodies, ways of responding to it with awareness rather than aversion, of creating and dancing in the space that is revealed. Removal of earlier forms and themes, and demonstration of the uncertainty of previous certainties, may allow for attention to reveal new freedoms and new forms – tentative, almost formless, arising wraith-like from new understanding. A distinction perhaps being that these new forms are often more self-conscious, more impermanent and more self-questioning, even in their sometimes in-your-face adolescent brashness, than were their more magisterial predecessors.

I shall try to follow contemporary traces of emptiness, both privative but also more positive, through the various branches of artistic practice. This is a personal survey and inevitably much that immediately springs to the minds of readers may be overlooked in a necessarily brief trawl through a vast ocean, with no chart but a search for echoes of emptiness. In many cases we are journeying along with the artists and have not the benefit of hindsight to draw out authoritative trends, schools and groupings within which to make the track more definitive and less a mere list of individual responses to emptiness. I make some attempt for the purpose of clarity to separate different practices, even while acknowledging that this is not really a successful method. One of the outstanding features of contemporary arts practice is the blurring of boundaries between disciplines that once were separated: the proscenium arch comes down, the frame is removed, the viewer is invited into the process; art and word, music and dance, and sculpture interweave. So there are many twists and turns and back-trackings on the journey, for which I ask the reader's patience and participation as the text transgresses its division into genres. The map is not the territory.

A forerunner in the culture of the imagination that contains echoes of emptiness is the Romantic notion of the Sublime. Traditionally considered as the highest of the high, that which is beyond comparison, the unbounded or undetermined, it has come to stand for experience that exceeds our perceptual or imaginative grasp, and marks the limit of reason or comprehension. The Sublime contains an excessive factor beyond the beautiful that brings terror as well as delight as it assails the safety of the self. The term became closely associated with the Romantic movement when it was used to explore the incommensurability of experience, reason and description. It stands for the undecidable, indeterminate and unpresentable. Here it is often an expression associated with transcendence, as in the well-known quotation from Wordsworth's 'Tintern Abbey':

> . . . a sense sublime
> Of something far more deeply interfused,
> Whose dwelling is the light of setting suns . . .

Yet the Sublime today has also come to bear different meanings. 'The postmodern sublime, one might say, is defined not by its intimations of transcendence but rather by its confirmation of immanence';[2] an immanence, however, that overwhelms the individual. As the American abstract artist Barnett Newman wrote: 'The sublime is NOW', in all its instant multiplicity, its complexity and its richness. According to Jean-François Lyotard, Newman was not thinking of 'now' as the present instant, but a now that, rather than being constituted by consciousness, is a stranger to consciousness; it is what dismantles and decomposes consciousness. It concerns an event in a sense that expresses the question 'Is it happening?', which precedes any sense of reasoning about what is happening and includes the possibility of nothing happening. Lyotard sees Cézanne as demonstrating this in his oeuvre, being that of 'an artist attempting to respond to the question: what is a painting?'[3]

It would seem that the territory of the contemporary Sublime concerning the limits of representation overlaps that of emptiness. Wallace Stevens describes the American Sublime (and is it critical or complimentary?) as:

> The empty spirit
> In vacant space.

In an essay on the contemporary Sublime, the writer Geoff Dyer suggests that we have arrived at a vision of the Sublime today that is literal and absolute, indicating that it is impossible to go any further; that in a world stripped of transcendent values, we are drawn increasingly into that desert that Don DeLillo has described as 'a container for emptiness'.[4] Yet both desert and emptiness may hold many interpretations.

> Seen with attention it is not a lack but an opportunity, a magnifying glass for that which is overlooked in noisier situations: desert space is always a listener, its only voice a quiet so unbroken it hushes you, thereby making you fit to enter in . . . How delicious . . . to listen and be no one at all. A 'no one' brimful, an emptiness who has become what there is.[5]

Emptiness, like that desert, may be experienced as a lack to be filled quickly with distraction or, feeling the horror and vacuity of mindless agitation, may be seen as a potential space for clearing the mind and, by paying careful attention, discovering the complexity and beauty that exists in the desert clarity.

Stephen Batchelor has used the term 'Sublime' in his translation of verses of Nagarjuna relating to the two levels of truth:

> Without relying on convention
> You cannot disclose the sublime;
> Without intuiting the sublime
> You cannot experience freedom.

He suggests that the Buddha used words such as 'deathless', 'timeless' and 'unborn' to suggest the sublime, as metaphors, drawing from what one knows to explain what one cannot know. He further suggests that 'emptiness' is also a metaphor, the one that Nagarjuna chose to denote the Sublime; the intention being, perhaps, to evade the tendency to picture the sublime as any-thing that we may then reify as transcendent or 'other'. 'The sublime', Batchelor says, 'may be beyond the grasp of concepts or language, but it is only ever encountered deep within the pulsing heart of what is happening here and now.'[6]

If we follow through completely to the emptiness of emptiness, the illusion of illusion, we can discover what remains – an experience, a way. The *via negativa* alone is no more valid than positive affirmation. It is in the dialectic of saying and unsaying that we may find pointers to the ineffable way that is beyond both positive and negative, transcendence and immanence. It is notable that mystics and artists found this way not through theory or orthodoxy, but through individual experience.

Before engaging with artistic practice in the contemporary West, let us also take another detour to the East, a revisiting of the way, *Tao* and *Do*, with specific reference to painting and poetry. As Marcel Conche noted, a different foundation for thought and art from that of Western traditions now provides themes that resonate with our contemporary concerns. There are some in contemporary Western artistic fields whose practice, and it has been a long, hard practice, has risen from the traditional Oriental sources that now bring them into alignment with the indeterminate philosophy and science of the contemporary world. Gary Snyder brought academic familiarity with Eastern painting and Chinese and Japanese poetry together with an outdoor childhood, mountain climbing, meditation experience and hard labour in trail crews in the wilderness of the western USA to forge a poetry that expresses this same mixture of presence, the emptiness behind all endeavour and attention to the hard minutiae of daily life. The French artist Fabienne Verdier has written of her long apprenticeship with a Chinese master of painting to achieve the momentary spontaneity that comes only from long practice and self-transformation. In both their works, emptiness sings.[7]

Yet beyond these and a few other exemplars, in most of the fields of contemporary and modern Western art, though the end point is similar – an acknowledgement of emptiness and an understanding of process along with the deconstruction of the object – this has come about in ways other than the traditional practices of understanding and self-transformation of Eastern traditions. Contemporary physics and contemporary art have undergone the same revolution, and both have come to speak easily in terms of energy and process. The rifts between subject and object, image and phenomenon, are splits that Western modernity has been seeking hard to breach. And as François Jullien noted: 'Painting and Physics understand each other especially regarding the operative characteristics of the void.'[8] Paradoxically, the very science that was more easily accommodated and encouraged within the Western viewpoint has challenged the philosophies of presence that encouraged it, leading it to views more easily accommodated within the Eastern outlook. Western artforms lacking the long centuries of the alignment of humans and world through the intentionality of breath-energy, and the concept of practices of attention to harmonize oneself with such energy, have had a longer journey to travel in order to deal with this changed landscape of thought. The resonances of emptiness echoing through contemporary arts may often be said to be the relative and nihilistic emptiness of which Nishitani speaks, rather than the absolute emptiness that is both emptiness *and* fullness.

### THE EMPTY WORD

Is the clarity, the simplicity, an arriving
Or an emptying out?
Jack Gilbert, 'The Answer'

George Steiner sees the West as being in the time of the 'after-Word' and the loss of 'real presences': indeed, in a time when the journey must go through 'real absence'. He dates the beginning of the crisis of the word to the poet Stéphane Mallarmé, who began the journey of dissociating poetic language from external reference, along with Arthur Rimbaud's deconstruction of the position of the self, the first person singular, with his statement '*Je est un autre*' ('I is another'). According to Steiner, this distribution of the self, the overthrow of naive correspondence between word and the empirical world, and between public enunciation and what is actually being said, was then accentuated by psychoanalysis. These movements and their implications 'splinter the foundations of the Hebraic-Hellenic-Cartesian edifice in which the *ratio* and the psychology of the Western communicative tradition had lodged'.[9] Steiner likens Mallarmé's repudiation of the validity of linguistic reference to Heisenberg's uncovering of uncertainty in physics. 'The truth of the word', he says, 'is the absence of the world' – in Mallarmé's own words, '*l'absence de toute rose*' (the absence of all rose); a step that takes us towards nihilism.

However, once we have realized that what words refer to are other words, and that it is in the linguistic system alone that we may find freedom of construction and deconstruction, understanding that words do not refer to a higher, better order hidden behind a reality of which it is a representation, we may return to a true freedom. In Heidegger's statement that language speaks itself, Steiner sees the first step out of nihilism into a different presence, one that does not require the patronage of anything more real.

> Enfranchised from the servitude of representation, purged of the lies, imprecisions and utilitarian dross which this servitude has brought with it, the 'word-world' can, via poetry and the poetics of thought in philosophy, resume its magical, its formal and categorical infinity.[10]

Such freedom, he believes, would aspire more to the condition of music. It is a process of abstraction, one that is perhaps more familiar in contemporary visual art. He illustrates this with the figures of Alberto Giacometti and the prose of Samuel Beckett.

Yet we must not ignore a divergent trend, one that challenges such abstraction and embodies itself in physicality – of the lived human body and of landscape. This, as we have seen, is a way closer to the Eastern tradition. It is also a recurring trope in Western art practice. The real presence, whose absence Steiner so mourns, is not absent from a Chinese painting, a Japanese haiku. It is there, quietly but surely, in a naturalistic immanence that finds in the subject presented a whole world of relationship, reference and meaning. Yet in both cases the work of art creates something out of emptiness. If the understanding of emptiness as potential comes more easily to the Eastern tradition, it has to be worked for harder by the modern and postmodern Western one. 'Deep inside every "art-act" lies the dream of an absolute leap out of nothing.'[11] Out of the emptiness that is both lack and possibility, the art-act creates. This dialectic between emptiness and form plays out in all the arts: as music comes out of silence, abstract art attempts to make visible the invisible world and words stripped of their absolute reference still attempt to point to the moon. It is finally, according to Steiner, an existential project:

> Responding to the poem, to the piece of music, to the painting, we re-enact, within the limits of our own lesser creativity, the two defining moments of our existential presence in the world: that of the coming into being where nothing was, where nothing could have continued to be, and that of the enormity of death.[12]

Often emptiness in the West enters by way of lack and reduction, as a response to the acknowledgement of death and absurdity. One thinks again of Beckett, of Mallarmé, of

Giacometti. It is found, too, in the breaking up of wholes, the loss of substance:

> What would one day be called 'the modern' was, at least as far as its sharpest and most hidden point is concerned, a legacy of the Buddha. Seeing things as so many aggregates and dismantling them. Then dismantling the elements split off from the aggregates, insofar as they too are aggregates. And so on and on in dizzying succession . . . Emptying of every substance from within . . . Seeing the world as a landscape of interlocking cogs.[13]

T. S. Eliot shows us emptiness in both aspects, privative and positive: privative, for example, in 'The Hollow Men', then in more redemptive fashion through the Indian influence of the 'Fire Sermon' in *The Waste Land*, which ends with its uneasy 'Shantih, shantih, shantih'. Finally he comes to a more positive interpretation at the end of the *Four Quartets* in 'Little Gidding', where the end is still the beginning, yet we may know our place for the first time and, echoing, Julian of Norwich, 'All shall be well', and the fire and the rose may be united.

Eliot writes, too, of the practices of emptiness and attention, of knowledge that imposes a pattern preventing us from seeing that every moment is a new pattern, and he challenges us to respond freshly. At the end of part III of 'East Coker', he makes a response to St John of the Cross, writing of the way of ignorance and the way of dispossession, where all you know is what you do not know, 'And where you are is where you are not'. The act of emptying enables the experience of freedom. Only through such paradox can Eliot express the moment between non-being and being, the moment in the rose garden when the hidden laughter is heard, the stillness that moves as the Chinese jar moves perpetually in its stillness, and the hidden light. For words, even his, cannot bear the strain, and slip and perish under the burden.

In a letter in 1967 Samuel Beckett, whose plays have been called 'hymns to nothingness', wrote that if he were in the 'unenviable position of having to study my work' his points of departure would be the 'Naught is more real than nothing', and the '*Ubi nihil vales, ibi nihil velis*' (Want nothing where you are worth nothing) that are both to be found in *Murphy* and describes them as 'neither very rational'.[14] And from the Addenda in *Watt*, the lines that seem to describe so much of Beckett's work ask us who can 'weigh absence in a scale' or 'nothingness in words enclose?'

It was fascinating that when I met Professor James Knowlson, Beckett's biographer and the creator of his archive at Reading University, and I was trying to explain my project to him, speaking of the ambiguous etymology of the Sanskrit term commonly translated as emptiness, *sunyata*, from the swelling of the seed, he immediately referenced Beckett's use of the word 'dehiscence'. In *Dream of Fair to Middling Women*, Beckett's character Belacqua applied this term to the painting of Rembrandt, speaking of:

> a disfaction, a désuni, an Ungebund, a flottement . . . a disaggregating, a disintegrating, and efflorescence, a breakdown and multiplication of tissue, the corrosive groundswell of Art.

And again, on the same page:

> I think of Beethofen [sic] . . . into the body of the musical statement he incorporates a punctuation of dehiscence, flottements, the coherence gone to pieces, the continuity bitched to hell because the units of continuity have abdicated their unity, they have gone multiple, they fall apart.[15]

Dehiscence is a biological term referring to the spontaneous opening at maturity of a plant structure to release its contents: loss and possibility. It also has a medical meaning as in a rupture of a surgical wound, or of an organ or structure to discharge its contents. A third meaning relates to a problem in the ear that causes vertigo. Another fascinating resonance of emptiness, perhaps?

From the wordiness of his early works, Beckett's later work, like Giacometti's figures, became slighter and slighter yet deeper and deeper, gaining meaning from the silence around the words as much as from the words themselves. He said of *Waiting for Godot* that silence was waiting to flood into the play like water into a sinking ship.[16] He also said of this work that it was a play that strived above all to evade definition.

Beckett's work has been considered as writing that comes closest to music. Every word, he said, is like an unnecessary stain on silence. Yet apparently he also said that he wanted to leave behind 'a stain on silence' and, in a tribute to his friend, the painter Avigdor Arikha spoke of Beckett's work approvingly as 'deep marks to show a stain on silence'. Such ambiguity is perhaps consistent for a man striving to evade definition and system.

As the linearity of narrative fails to reflect the simultaneity of experience, the written word, in both fiction and drama, may be the least telling of the arts described here. Blurring the boundaries between poetry, drama and prose, Beckett's later works leave narrative behind, replacing it

by attempts of consciousness to perceive, comprehend, or create first a life, then a more or less stable, static image, an essence, failing at the latter no less often than at the former.[17]

As one of Beckett's characters says, 'No need of a story, a story is not compulsory, just a life, that's the mistake I made, one of the mistakes, to have wanted a story for myself whereas life alone is enough.'[18] Perhaps the fact that life alone *is* enough explains why, despite the privative take on nothingness, the stains on silence bear the slightest tinge of redemption, as in the remembered moment of bliss in the punt from *Krapp's Last Tape*, Winnie's *Happy Days* and even the exhortation to 'Fail again. Fail better.'

What is left in the later work is what S. Contarski calls '"nothing", incorporeal consciousness perhaps', and Beckett is surely the writer who enacts best the play of emptiness and form. Content and form appear indivisible as he explores the human imagination, examining 'the diaphanous membrane separating inside from outside, perception from imagination, self from others, narrative from experience, "neither" wholly the one nor wholly the other' in a manner that has been likened to the complementarity of waves and particles.[19] One of Beckett's most 'empty' writings, a short piece that hovers between prose and poetry, and has indeed been printed with and without line endings, *Neither*, was dedicated to the composer Morton Feldman, whose own work inhabits similar regions of sound. Two lines will perhaps serve to illustrate how this piece enacts inbetweenness and resonates with many of the concerns I am attempting to delineate:

> to and fro in shadow from inner to outershadow
> from impenetrable self of impenetrable unself by way
> of neither[20]

Whereas Beckett strove to match his form to the content of his vision, others have expressed new vision within more traditional forms. In the afterword to his version of Rainer Maria Rilke's *Sonnets to Orpheus*, the poet Don Patterson writes that he started his version of Rilke's sonnets in response to his own long and sometimes painful conversion to scientific materialism. He found that the loss of God, and especially the

leaving behind of 'everything from ghost, soul and super-
stition to the seductive appeals of essentialism, humanism and
the Anthropic Principle – end of intelligent design . . . left the
room terribly quiet and empty'.[21] In that emptiness of loss he
sought a text as an aide-memoire to what he now held to be
most true. This he found in Rilke's *Sonnets*, which he feels
'insist on sheer wondering enquiry as the central sane human
activity', along with Rilke's acknowledgement of the error of
thinking of any afterlife as more extraordinary than finding
ourselves alive here and now. Such projection of ourselves into
the future, beyond our present life, warps our response-ability
and our responsibility to the present. Patterson sees Orpheus
standing for Rilke as the symbol of this duality between
knowledge of death and of the living present – this duality
that we find in so many of the writers, philosophers and artists
mentioned above, from Heidegger to Beckett. In the face of
emptiness, man can sing.

This afterword underlines for me the understanding of
emptiness experienced throughout Rilke's work. The governing
insight of Rilke's poetry, Patterson explains, is his understanding of man as unique in his conscious foreknowledge of his own
death, which leads him always into the future, into a narrative,
which paradoxically ignores that its plot or shape is informed
and made possible by death. Religion that ignores death or sees
a future beyond this life eradicates our attention from the 'real'
wonder of the human experience, what Rilke wonderfully
describes as 'I flow – I am.' Orpheus stands for the resolution
of this split between life and death – the true singer – bridging
the divide between 'breathing present and atemporal eternity'.[22]
This to me seems similar to bridging the gap – in Buddhist
terms – between the two truths, or two ways of knowing, ultimate and conventional, emptiness and dependent origination,
or in experiential terms between emptiness of ultimate knowledge and our present life. A life in which for Rilke humans, as

the only conscious singers, have a duty to bear witness and to praise; praise that seems close to the thinking that is thanking of Heidegger.

> Why do we have to be human?
> Because simply to be here is so much
> Because what is here seems to need us.[23]

Patterson shows his own understanding of poetry as emblematic of process and emptiness in his T. S. Eliot Lecture of 2004:

> I've always felt that every morning the poet should stand at the window and remember that nothing that they see, not a bird or stone, has in its possession the name they give it.

He continues:

> when we allow silence to reclaim those objects and things of the world, when we allow the words to fall away from them – they reassume their own genius, and repossess something of their mystery, their infinite possibility.[24]

Silence, he feels, is thus the first thing that the poet in the act of composition should always observe and honour. Such awareness of contingency and silence allows language to become aware of itself, to use new metaphors to reignite the dead ones through which we habitually speak.

I have mentioned earlier the virtually inevitable linearity of narrative that is perhaps one of the main reasons for the scarcity of the resonance emptiness in the novel; then I read an essay by Milan Kundera that seemed to supply another. He points out the interesting fact of the lack of progeny of the protagonists of major novels. He contends that the novel as the product of the modern era, in which man is the only subject and the ground for everything, separates out the individual and makes him the centre of everything. When he dies the novel is ended. Should the story go on after the end of the individual life, it means that a

> life is not an independent entity; it means it is unfinished, unfulfilled; it means there is something utterly concrete and earthly into which the individual blends, agrees to blend, consents to be lost in: family, posterity, tribe, nation. It means that the individual person, as 'ground for everything', is an illusion, a gamble, the dream of a few European centuries.[25]

The illusion of the idea of the individual as a ground for everything is the song of emptiness, a song that the novel rarely sings – rarely, but not never. The essay quoted above is a consideration of Gabriel García Márquez's novel *One Hundred Years of Solitude* (1967), a work that Kundera considers rises above such thoughts: the centre of attention being no longer an individual, but a procession of individuals, each of them 'merely the brief flash of a sunbeam on the swell of a river', none of them staying for long at the centre of the story. I think that since this novel there have been others that have attempted to express the reality of a procession of individuals and shift the focus from the individual story to that of a network of relationships. Indeed, also earlier, John Steinbeck's *Cannery Row* (1945) could stand as an ecological novel, bringing the same understanding that Steinbeck applied to the tide pools of the Sea of Cortez to the human life of the Monterey waterfront. There are many other similar examples, but more, I think, in the last decades than previously.

Certainly the beginning of the twentieth century saw the results of the loss of authority and the awareness of contingency in philosophy extend to fiction. If God was dead, so too was the authoritative voice of the reliable narrator. Just as Freud had demonstrated the power of the unconscious and the loss of the governor self, so the self in literature also appeared fragmented into the stream of consciousness so beautifully played out in the novels of Virginia Woolf and James Joyce. Yet these, particularly in the case of *Finnegans Wake*, have come to be seen as somewhat blind alleys in the history of literature; the extent of their formal experimentation has few followers today. Looking back at Woolf's work, her courage and experimentation still astonish over the years. Her most individual works, *To the Lighthouse*, *The Waves* and *Between the Acts*, blur the boundaries between prose, poetry and drama. Perhaps the least mentioned, the posthumous *Between the Acts* (1941) illustrates aspects of my theme most closely. The selves presented, both real and those of the pageant featured in the novel, are all 'orts, scraps and fragments'. The book itself, as described in the wonderful recent introduction by Jackie Kaye, is 'an ode to unity and disunity' in which everything happens 'in the margins, the borders, between the acts'. It plays with the tension between the visible and invisible, real and unreal, past and present, actor and audience, and finally in two wonderfully brave exhortations, first asks us to 'try ten minutes of present time', bringing all the divisions together, appearance and reality, in experience as is, in the moment; then again, to 'break the rhythm and forget the rhyme. And calmly consider ourselves. Ourselves.' As the players in the pageant hold up mirrors to the audience, so the writer holds up a mirror to her readers. There is even among the pages of the novel an important reference to silence and source, wrapped in a description of a painting referred to several times in the text:

> Empty, empty, empty; silent, silent, silent. The room was a shell, singing of what was before time was; a vase stood in the heart of the house, alabaster smooth, cold, holding the still distilled essence of emptiness, silence.[26]

Samuel Beckett, whose early novels followed on stylistically from James Joyce, gradually concluded that this style of complexity and elaboration was not his own road, and turned to the path of ever-increasing abstraction and reduction, in his later work also blurring the boundaries between prose, poetry, music and drama. The novel, though, which is despite all news to the contrary alive and kicking, is with its narrative demands perhaps the most formally resistant artistic practice to the new paradigms of science and theory. This may, of course, be because it has the most facility to address such changes in its content, if not its form. The same applies, I think, to drama. Only Beckett seems to stand out as one who has united form and content on the stage to sing of emptiness.

A few writers do manage to address the indefinability and emptiness at the heart of identity in the content and context of more traditional individual stories. A Swiss professor of philosophy, who writes under the pen name Pascal Mercier, in *Perlmann's Silence* and *Night Train to Lisbon* uses the novel form to explore contingency and the slipperiness of identity. Within a traditional narrative structure he investigates the interdependence of identity and narrative, and the function of language and narrative, both explicitly and implicitly in the construction of identity, doing so in fascinating intertwinings of story and philosophy that present identity in a far from usual manner. As one of his characters states:

> one must clearly understand that the narrating self is none other than the narrated stories. Apart from the stories there is nothing. Or rather, no one . . . Most people find that a shocking assertion. I've never understood why. I find it quite pleasant that that's how it is. Somehow . . . liberating.[27]

On the other hand, in a fascinating manifesto arguing for the contemporary power and importance of incorporating reality into all forms of media, David Shields notes the loss of importance of plot and narrative, and points to collage, 'the art of reassembling fragments of preexisting images in such a way as to form a new image', as the major innovation in the art of the twentieth century. Collage, he sees as 'a demonstration of the many becoming the one, with the one never fully resolved because of the many that continue to impinge on it'. He suggests that today the most compelling creative energies are to be found in non-fiction. In search of epiphany and reality, he extols the virtues of the essay as experiment and open-ended journey, a direct response to life. In particular he points to the lyric essay, which he suggests asks and embodies what happens when an essay ceases to act like an essay and begins to act like a poem.

> Facts quicken, multiply, change shape, elude us, and bombard our lives with increasingly suspicious promises. The hybrid shape-shifting, ambiguous nature of lyric essays makes a flow-chart of our experiences of the world. No longer able to depend on canonical literature, we journey increasingly across boundaries, along borders, into fringes, and finally through our yearnings to quest, where only more questions are found; through our primal senses, where we record every wonder; through our own burning hearts, where we know better.[28]

Certainly as a response to the lived reality of contemporary experience such a mixture of experienced reality, fragmentation, improvisation and collage, while fitting the form of the lyric essay, is also to be found among all the fields of art practice. The writer Terry Tempest Williams beseeched the ocean to 'Give me one wild word' to help her retrieve the poetry she had lost after the 9/11 disaster and to help her in her subsequent political involvement, 'And the word the ocean rolled back to me was "mosaic".'[29]

Freed from the necessity of narrative, experience may fragment, compress and recompose, the gaps between the shards allowed to show through, the silence between the words allowed to speak, the space of the white paper gleaming between the type. Perhaps this is the true reason why emptiness occurs most frequently in poetry rather than prose, and that it is the most poetic of prose writers that sing of emptiness most clearly.

## THE VISIBLE AND INVISIBLE

It's only in darkness you can see the light, only
From emptiness that things start to fill
Charles Wright, 'Looking Around'

In the visual arts there has been a progressive loss of the object and a breaking down of the perspective and position of both artist and viewer. Cubism deconstructed the conventional view of things, gave a multi-perspectival view and deformed, if not actually broke down, the barrier between subject and object. Abstract Expressionism furthered the project. Representation was replaced by presentation, presentation by participation. From the middle of the twentieth century onwards the 'dematerialization of the art object' was accelerated in the explosion of conceptual art, happenings, installation, performance and even land art. All these genres presented 'various efforts toward dematerialization and the embrace of the impermanent, the ephemeral, the temporal, the formless, the contingent and the immaterial'.[30] This involved both the breaking down of the actual subject-matter and a more subtle, emotional approach. Just as George Steiner pointed to Beckett and Giacometti as representing a movement away from representation, so Jean-Paul Sartre wrote of the

profound rupture with classicism that Giacometti enacted, precisely in his conception of the rapport between statue and space: a space no longer measurable and divided, but imaginary and so absolute.

Sartre asked:

> How to paint emptiness? Before Giacometti it seemed that no one would attempt it. For five hundred years, pictures were full to bursting: the force of the universe inhabited them. With his canvasses, Giacometti begins to expel the world.[31]

These practices also questioned the value of the artist's unique subjectivity, and placed meaning in the encounter, the experience produced by the viewer's confrontation with the work. Contemporary art bursts out of the frame, engages and calls for attention, for participation, even when it seems to alienate. Constantly it asks us to see the world in a new way. A composer, John Luther Adams, in describing his approach to music, writes:

> One of the defining currents of twentieth-century painting was the movement away from the detached viewpoint of perspective and its illusions of receding depth, toward a new emphasis on color and surface.[32]

He likens this to a movement in music away from the sequential development of relationships between sounds to an emphasis on the inherent qualities of the sounds themselves heard in the present moment. Both exemplify a movement away from linear narrative and perspective. Adams suggests that perspective is a way of removing ourselves from experience. Painting that has no fixed perspective fails to tell us where we are standing, and invites us to travel freely within its ambiguous space; it 'creates a presence that demands our participation'.[33] The curator Lee Joon, in his essay accompanying the Seoul exhibition 'The Void in Korean Art' in 2007, suggests that 'the more space is allotted to void, the more important the viewer's role becomes.'[34] Viewers must actively engage in that space of emptiness. One thinks of the black canvases of Ad Reinhardt, of Robert Rauschenberg's white paintings, of Yves Klein's ultramarine, of Barnett Newman's 'zips', and perhaps most of all of the floating colour fields of Mark Rothko, and then, beyond the canvas, of the experiential encounters of James Turrell and Olafur Eliasson.

Speaking of a desired effect in music, Adams writes of the phenomenon of visual space called *ganzfeld* in which, immersed in pure colour, the viewer loses all sense of distance and direction.[35] This phenomenon has been wonderfully explored by James Turrell, one of the most interesting contemporary artists and one of several whose work, while most challenging us to alter our ways of seeing, is yet most grounded in the interface of perception and the natural world. 'The world is not a predetermined given set of facts; we construct the world with our observations.'[36] So says Turrell who has, for the last 25 years, been sculpting out the inside of an extinct volcano in the Arizona high desert in order to form sky-watching chambers and experiential vantage points on the curvature of space. It is the magnum opus that will encapsulate all of Turrell's work which, within and without galleries, sculpts light, and offers experiences that warp, question and expand our normal perception. Turrell offers a meditative experience of emptiness that alters perception. One of the pieces in a recent exhibition entitled *Dhatu* (2010)

yields an emptiness filled with light that allows the viewer to feel its physicality. Light like this is seen rarely with the eyes open yet it is familiar to that which can be apprehended with the eyes closed in lucid dream, deep meditation and near death experiences.[37]

Another work of behind-the-eye vision involves the viewer spending time in a metal capsule, lying flat, isolated in a white space that then is filled with sound and colour. By combining intense colour with sound, the intent is to alter the brain-wave frequencies of participants. The work is called *Bindu Shards*, Bindu being a sacred symbol of the cosmos in its unmanifest state. It is held to be the point that begins creation, where unity becomes manifest in the many. It is also a tantric term used in connection with the energies of the subtle body. Other recurring works of Turrell's, as with his plans for Roden Crater, involve the natural world, setting up sky-watching spaces in which lighting and framing help to intensify the experience of paying bare attention to the ever-changing sky.

Eliasson also makes use of the natural world to offer contemplative sensory experiences within an art framework in such works as *Take Your Time* (2007) and *The Weather Project* (2003). *Take Your Time* offered a series of experiences that enfolded the viewer in the work. For example: inside a drum of white screens, changing colours surrounded, encircled and overwhelmed the viewer. If you took your time in this environment, you could sense how variously the different colours made you feel. To be drenched in blue was a wholly different experience from being soaked in pink, or immersed in clear white. Sadly, when I was there, the majority of people failed to take the necessary time to fully appreciate the sensory and emotional experience, rushing on to the next offering, a little confused as to what was happening, and unwilling to experience the seeming emptiness. Such art, such emptiness, asks for a different response from that to a given object, the single perspective. Eliasson has talked of the introspective aspects and intentions of work like this: 'what I sometimes call the introspective quality of seeing: you see whatever you're looking at, but you also see the way you're seeing'.[38] This is also described as a major part of insight meditation. In language common to that of meditation, he also speaks of the co-arising of mind and body, perception and cognition.

Grounded in the reality of the natural world yet far from using mere representation, other artists employ the natural in ways that demonstrate the creation of work from space and from emptiness. The transience of Andy Goldsworthy's interventions in the natural world, the traces of Richard Long's passage through the landscape, Hamish Fulton's headline to his webpage 'Only Art Resulting from the Experience (of Individual Walks)', all pay tribute to the indivisibility of experience and creation in impermanent performance.

While Goldsworthy, Eliasson and Turrell use light and the natural world to produce and enhance experience and participation, other artists use the practice of their art to draw attention to attention itself rather than to any object, showing the dialogue between emptiness and formation in practices of attention that are both focused and abstract. There are so very many names that could be mentioned here. Agnes Martin, Vija Celmins, Robert Irwin, Richard Tuttle, Rachel Whiteread – I hope each reader will think of their own. Bill Viola's groundbreaking work, particularly in slowing down process, has traced on video and film the tracks of emptiness and silence. Who could fail to find these in small scale in such works as *Catherine's Room*, and on the larger screen in his elemental explorations of water, fire and air?

Then there is Anselm Kiefer. In the film biography *Over Your Cities Grass Will Grow,* motifs of sea and books symbolize the ability to be empty and capable of being filled. In one extraordinarily telling scene, Kiefer is speaking of how little we know despite all the advances of science, saying that the core (of life?) is a vacuum, a void; yet he admits to being drawn forwards by the 'puppet of beauty', and as he is speaking a young boy, possibly his son, runs behind him, visible to the camera but holding his hands in front of his face and pretending he cannot be seen. The contrast between the words of emptiness, the lure of beauty and the living presence of a mischievous member of the next generation is a moment of simultaneity that the director could surely never have hoped for.

A recent suite of works by Kiefer, *Das Meeres und der Liebe Wellen* (The Waves of Sea and Love, 2011), further expresses his understanding of emptiness. In the accompanying exhibition catalogue there is a translation of a lecture he gave earlier in the year. Writing of Rimbaud's poem 'Marine', he likens it to Mallarmé in giving:

> the feeling of abolishing meaning by silencing words, rendering language mute in order to draw closer to silence . . . For just as language cannot apprehend nothingness, nothingness cannot be expressed except in language.

The most interesting moment, he believes, is that in which the subject moves into abstraction, language into silence: 'A moment that sits on an intangible frontier that expresses the struggle against the representation of nothingness and of nothingness itself.'[39] Kiefer sees the totally abstract (and here he references a work by Donald Judd) as empty not of something, but empty from their inception; as 'pure design, they do not express emptiness as a virtual and spiritual entity'. Against such privative emptiness he chooses a work by Walter De Maria, *Vertical Earth Kilometer,* as expressing the fertile aspect of emptiness. Similarly, on the verbal knife-edge between meaning and abstraction, 'Rimbaud's poetry,' he says, 'and also to an even greater extent Mallarmé's, is absolutely aimed at nothingness, which is the absolute par excellence.'[40] The more knowledge we acquire, he believes, 'the wider the doors of the unknown stand open.'[41] Kiefer ends the essay by saying that the sole real things in our lives are art and poetry, and quotes from

Rilke's *Sonnets to Orpheus* the lines: 'To the earth, say "I flow", To the water, say "I am"', and these lines are inscribed on one of his *Das Meeres* works.

The cultural historian Homi Bhabha has written an essay on the work of Anish Kapoor entitled 'Making Emptiness', opening it with a quotation from the psychologist Wilfred Bion: 'Inability to tolerate empty space limits the amount of space available.' Bhabha continues:

> It may be the most valuable insight into Anish Kapoor's work to suggest that the presence of an object can render a space more empty than mere vacancy could ever envisage. This quality of an excessive engendering emptiness is everywhere visible in his work.[42]

In a way that is reminiscent of traditional Chinese thought, Kapoor sees that his role as an artist is not to *be* expressive, saying that he is without a message, but to *bring to* expression. He speaks of this as a process that is associated with contrary yet correlated forces of withdrawal and disclosure. With his enormous tower for London that will remain as a memento long after the Olympic Games it was commissioned to celebrate, Kapoor is taking these views into the mainstream. Speaking of this, the engineer for the project said, 'it takes uncertainty as a given'. In an article about it, this uncertainty is contrasted to the certainty of the games, where races have a form – a beginning, middle and end – while above the tower 'tells a different story: of fluidity, change and divergence of viewpoints . . . that nothing is forever, but everything possible'.[43]

Before becoming an artist, Antony Gormley, whose enormous sculpture *Angel of the North* has also entered mainstream experience, spent considerable time with a teacher of insight, or vipassana meditation. This is a form of meditation that invites bare attention to the body, feelings and perception. His subsequent art is a body-based practice that radiates attention and stillness. Early works included leaden figures that were cast from plaster moulds of his own body. Thomas McEvilley, professionally an art historian and critic in addition to his encyclopaedic survey of ancient thought, speaking of these works, saw in them signs of both aspects of emptiness described throughout this book: the emptiness of lack and nihilism, and the emptiness of possibility. He noted 'the ambiguous emptiness, an emptiness that can be seen either as a sign of the spirit's triumphant escape or the tragic residue of a failed humanity'.[44] Perhaps it is a very European response that expresses these two aspects as either/or, rather than letting them resonate in their ambiguity.

In an interview with Pierre Tillett, Gormley speaks of his hollow bodies as tools carrying

> nothing else than emptiness, shadow, darkness, carrying the condition of embodiment. They each carry the condition we all know. All you have to do is shut your eyes when you are awake [and] you are in the place that the bodyforms and the bodycases carry.[45]

He agrees with his interviewer that this emptiness is like an energetic void, which is the condition of existence, and which animates the body – the *anima* of ancient philosophers.

In another interview in 2008 with the gallerist Hans Ulrich Obrist, Gormley suggests that for most of its history European art has been about picturing, and that with modernism it turned to interpretation and deconstruction. Currently, he thinks, there is a new phase 'in which art is about providing a place where the human subject is somehow able to concentrate on his/her own being'.[46] He mentions Eliasson and *Take Your Time* in this context. In this paradigm, 'subjective experience of space time, the condition of life, rather than being in some sense the assumed background condition for refined perceptions of the object, now becomes a landscape in itself.' He speaks of a movement from the theatrical forms of participation of 1960s happenings to the bare attention called forth by such works as those of Eliasson, Richard Serra's wall projects and Walter De Maria's lightning fields.

If there is one thread through the practices of all these so different artists it is that of attention. Turrell comes from a Quaker background with its traditions of speaking out of silence; Gormley spent much time practising meditation; and Kapoor connects with Indian traditions. Earlier one could single out the almost lifelong obsession of Cézanne with Montagne Sainte-Victoire, constructed, deconstructed, never seen as identical; and also the purity of sight and form that Brancusi obtained, along with his joy in the songs of the Tibetan saint and hermit Milarepa. And surely emptiness *sive* fullness sings from the suffused colour of Mark Rothko's canvasses.

Even these, however, rely upon actual artefacts, pieces of stone and canvasses that bear lasting marks. It is indicative of the trend in contemporary art that London's Tate Modern is opening a new space for performative, multimedia and film works. Film, like the novel and drama, is largely and usually a narrative-based form, and traces of emptiness are rare and, outside art galleries, are usually concerned with content and story rather than form. The few narrative films that have sung emptiness to me, such as *Why Has Bodhidharma Left for the East? Spring, Summer, Autumn, Winter . . . and Spring* come from Eastern cultures; they are films that tell their stories against an implicit understanding of emptiness. From the West I can think only of the recent season of filmed performances of Beckett's oeuvre and of *Le Quatro Volte* (2000–02), a film that significantly rolls almost entirely without words in its portrayal of life in Calabria, attempting the perspective of men, goats, trees and minerals in a manner that hesitates to prefer any one, and by so doing presents a slow, strange and rich depiction. Within the space of the gallery, however, liberated from the necessity and linearity of plot, many video pieces, especially those of Bill Viola, spring immediately to mind, which are freed from the necessity of narrative, and illustrate ideas and visions of emptiness.

Despite the fact that the development of photographic process is often cited as a reason for the loss of figuration in painting as it took over the project of realistic representation, in contemporary still photographic work itself we may frequently follow traces of emptiness. There are photographers like Michael Kenna whose work appears steeped in the Chinese artistic philosophy described earlier, where space and subject, emptiness and form, coexist in a mutual dialogue. There are others such as Todd Hido, whose pictures equally suggest uncertainty and contingency in a more narrative form. Other photographers that spring to mind in the context of emptiness also come from traditions steeped in Buddhist thought. The photographs of Hiroshi Sugimoto are a great demonstration of the way close attention can make the familiar strange, often inhabiting that fertile, liminal area between representation and abstraction. Somehow his seascapes are distinctly different from the large seascapes of Thomas Joshua Cooper, in which the matter if not the manner is similar. The Korean photographer Boo Moon also devoted a whole series to the liminal space between sea and sky, further subverted by snow, in his work entitled *Nakan*. Before this an earlier series was based on sky alone. Again on that cusp of subject and abstraction described as so fruitful by Anselm Kiefer, another Korean photographer, Bohnchang Koo, produces photographs of mysterious beauty and expression. One series I think of in particular is based on traces of ivy left on walls. In photographs of great delicacy, time, decay, nature and the human eye, and impermanence, are shown. The images of Masao Yamamoto also play with space and form, delicacy, humour and the unexpected in a way unusual to the Western imagination. All these artists allow for the space of emptiness, indeterminacy and openness behind the given image.

Yet other practitioners, whose work carries an explicit understanding of emptiness, have been directly influenced by Buddhist thought. Of Minor White, John Daido Loori and Stephen Batchelor, the last two are probably better known for their writings on Buddhist themes than for their photography. In an essay, 'Seeing the Light', from a volume on Buddhist influences in art, Batchelor mentions two themes that have constantly recurred in our journeys around emptiness – attention and collage. His practice of making collages out of found objects led him to realize that photographs too are found objects; the raw data of the image is given, then 'moments in the visual field', like the pieces of a collage, can be organized in the viewfinder to create an image. The attention and receptivity required for good image are ways of cultivating awareness and transforming perception. He cites Roland Barthes in *Camera Lucida*, making a link between the photograph and Buddhist ideas of emptiness and suchness in the way a photograph is a unique, unrepeatable event capturing the contingency and evanescence of the moment. 'In order to designate reality, Buddhism says *sunya*, the empty; but better still: *tathata*, the fact of being this, of being thus, of being so.' Yet casting aside specific Buddhist ideas as informing his practice directly, Batchelor says that photography, like meditation, is a tool for challenging the assumption that the world is just the way it appears at first sight.[47]

In Britain, rooted in the natural world yet travelling well beyond representation, I would also draw attention to the cameraless photography of Susan Derges and Garry Fabian Miller. In different ways, the first organic and overtly beautiful, the second more geometric and abstract, both artists attempt to capture process rather than representation, often by employing photographic practices that bypass the will of the photographer. Both are expressions of attention. Christian Marclay has used a lensless type of process, the cyanotype, also employed by both Derges and Miller, to make printed work that expresses time in static images, as well as in his now famous 24-hour film, *The Clock* (2010).

Many echoes of emptiness were evident in a recent trip to the San Francisco Museum of Modern Art. As I crossed the high, open walkway on the topmost floor, with its lattice floor through which the space beneath is revealed, I was presented with a sound sculpture, *Sonic Shadow*, by Bill Fontana. Ambient sounds, including those of the viewer's own passing, subtle movements of the air magnified by sensitive speakers and sensors, accompanied the viewer's passage. Invisible and intangible, their audibility made the space more apparent in what was described as 'a live acoustic translation of the architectural space'. In another part of the museum there was a 'scent sculpture'. The viewer was invited to stroke a painted alcove that then emitted the faint trace of wine on someone's breath – so evanescent as to be almost unnoticed. In another gallery an entire wall was painted indigo like the night sky, and marked with small, white crosses in tape and larger, three-dimensional, neon white letters and numbers that lit up in random sequence. The letters spelled out the names of towns in the United States that relate to nothing – Nada, Nameless, Not, Nonesuch, Dearth, Lostcity, Guess – and the figures showed their geographical locations. The work, by Peter Wegner, is titled *The United States of Nothing*, and the legend explains:

Pinpointing the latitude and longitude of American towns whose name refers to 'nothing', Wegner offers the paradox of marking locations that assert their own absence. America shifts, in this work, from a solidarity to something considerably more uncertain.[48]

I realize that there is so much I have not mentioned. I have barely spoken about Yves Klein, whose *The Void* and *The Leap Into the Void* illustrate the trajectory of his entire work; or about Martin Creed, whose Turner Prize-winning lights going on and off in an empty room might well stand as a metaphor for the ways of seeing emptiness, as lack or potential. I have also passed over in silence Rauschenberg's erasure of a work by Willem de Kooning. I have tried not to lose the sense of the development of the guiding idea of emptiness in a catalogue of examples, though as emptiness is a quality that is an aspect of all phenomena and of individual responses to this, there is a danger of presenting a list of examples that is both endless and disparate. There is a path, however, tracing from Brancusi's minimal forms, which draw attention to their surrounding space, through Barbara Hepworth's introduction of space in the form of holes in the figure, to Klein's empty room, through all the works described – actual, conceptual, performative and experiential – that draws attention to space, emptiness and imagination. I just hope that the discussion will have tweaked the lenses of your vision from a setting on substance to that of emptiness, and that it will invite experiences like my trip to the San Francisco Museum of Modern Art.

This was certainly the aim behind a conveyance of emptiness into the (almost) mainstream at the summer exhibition of a large public London gallery titled 'Invisible: Art about the Unseen, 1957–2012'. The curator suggested that the intention of all that was on show was to fire the imagination; that 'This is the best show that you will never see'. Klein, Cage, erasure and the Sublime were all referenced, even if they were not to be seen or heard. In particular, one phrase, used by the curator in his accompanying booklet, for me emphasized the importance of the show. He spoke of it as a challenge to 'the complacency of seeing'.[49] Artists that are philosophers of emptiness challenge the complacency not only of seeing, but also of listening and conventional thinking.

> . . . Except for the point, the still point,
> There would be no dance . . .
>
> T. S. Eliot, *Burnt Norton*

The history of music also shows that breaking down of structures we have seen in other fields. The traditional foundations of harmony in Western classical music became more and more sophisticated and stretched, until they finally broke down. The pivot akin to Mallarmé's rose would probably be the Tristan Chord of Wagner written in the years between 1857 and 1864. Claude Debussy (1862–1918) further destabilized the notion of harmony, leading to the atonalism of the Second Viennese School of Anton Webern and Arnold Schoenberg and (to a lesser extent) Alban Berg. The atonal universe has no centre. Alex Ross describes Webern writing ecstatically of being lost in a snowstorm and walking into a whiteness like 'a completely undifferentiated screen', and says that his music offered a similar experience for the ears.[50]

Later, as if frightened by such freedom, serialism reintroduced strict rules, and at this time too the predominance of Europe in the narrative comes towards its end, to be picked up and joined by the American story and its experimentation with jazz and space, and the West Coast exploration of non-European music. Minimalism, repetition, time-based writing, improvisation, jazz and exotic instrumentation, such as gamelan and the self-invented instruments of Harry Partch, are just a few of the ciphers of the new, pluralistic assaults upon previous orthodoxy.

The infamous 4′33″ silent piece by John Cage perhaps best epitomizes a musical concern with emptiness and contingency that is also demonstrated by his aleatoric music based on chance and the throwing of Taoist I Ching coins. Cage wrote, 'If you work with chance operations you're basically shifting – from the responsibility to choose to the responsibility to ask.' When asked if he was faithful to the answers he received he continued that when in the position of someone who would change something, he changed himself rather than the answers, and 'I have said that instead of self-expression, I'm involved in self-alteration.'[51] This carries echoes of Hadot's interpretation of early philosophy as a way of life, and it also bridges the division of performer and audience, for what occurs is an opportunity for the self-alteration of the audience as his work intends to engage the attentiveness of the audience as much as the concentration of the performer. He stated that

> the piece is not actually silent . . . it is full of sound, but sounds which I did not think of beforehand, which I hear for the first time the same time others hear. What we hear is determined by our own emptiness, our own receptivity; we receive to the extent we are empty to do so.[52]

In relation to the ambient sounds that occur in 4′33″, the cars from the street and audience coughs, he said that they might appear initially as interruptions, but if we engage in self-alteration, we will see them as enrichments.

Always interested in the idea of silence, Cage had visited the anechoic chamber at Harvard University, a room that was supposedly entirely silent. He found, however, that he heard two quiet sounds, the high one being that of his nervous system, and the low one that of his blood circulating. This impossibility and/or potentiality of silence matched his view of the all-white paintings of Robert Rauschenberg, where he saw how the uniformity of the canvas was always changed by alterations of shadow and light. Cage gave equal importance to both sound and silence, going so far as to suggest that since silence cannot be heard in terms of pitch, loudness or timbre, duration should be the fundamental characteristic of the material of music. Thus, he said: "There can be no right making of music that does not structure itself from the very roots of sound and silence – lengths of time."[53]

Cage attended classes with D. T. Suzuki and applied his understanding of the meditative mind as one in which the ego does not obstruct the reception of sensation and the images of dreams. As the psychologist Mark Epstein has described it, 'If you develop an ear for sounds that are musical it is like developing an ego. You begin to refuse sounds that are not musical and that way cut yourself off from a good deal of experience.'[54]

Cage's influence, both explicit and implicit, has been enormous. In music his ideas of duration, his uses of found sound and of aleatoric process, crop up commonly, and his influence has spread far beyond music into all the fields of art practice. In 2007 the British artist Tacita Dean invited Cage's partner, the dancer Merce Cunningham, to collaborate on a piece based on 4'33". Six performances of Cunningham's response to 4'33" were captured in six films entitled *Stillness,* in which the contrast and complementarity of stasis/movement reflects the sound/silence dialogue of the original. Further demonstrating the overlap of all the fields of art practice, a recent suite of paintings by the German artist Gerhard Richter is titled *Cage.* The artist, long interested in Cage's ideas about ambient sound and silence, was listening to his music while he worked on the paintings. Here, the sound/silence dialogue is reflected in that of painting and erasure, where the artist has painted several layers of paint, later erased by squeegee, brushing and scraping. Richter has said of them: 'I have nothing to say and I am saying it.'[55]

Another colleague of Cage's was Morton Feldman, who illustrates well this blurring between genres that is emblematic of the contemporary art scene. Feldman is noted for his relationships with painters almost more than with musicians. One of his best-known works is *Rothko Chapel,* which arose from a commission to write a suite of music for an interfaith chapel decorated with fourteen huge Rothko paintings in Houston, Texas. To illustrate the place of emptiness and attention in Feldman's work, I can do no better than quote from the programme notes accompanying a performance given by the San Francisco Symphony Orchestra in 2011.

> Silence gets its moments in Feldman's compositions, and he has a talent for framing it in a way that emphasizes its musical possibilities. But more striking still is his use of near-silence. Feldman is the ultimate 'low-talker' among composers, and he can make you strain to listen. When you have to work to hear somebody, you tend to pay undivided attention to what he or she is saying. So it is with Feldman's music: it demands your concentration, and it does not invite you to be a casual listener. The solo timpani, playing *pianississimo* at the outset of this work, gets things off to an entirely characteristic start. In fact, unless you have a direct view of the timpanist's mallets, you will probably be uncertain about when the piece actually does begin. At some point you will become aware that a sound is present, but you may suspect that it was already there before you perceived it. The piece is filled with attacks of that sort, both vocal and instrumental – of notes that emerge into audibility, of lines that are handed off among performers with seamless purity.

It continues, drawing attention to the contemplative mindfulness that Feldman requires and evokes from the audience:

The *Rothko Chapel* serves as a contemplative space, and Feldman's piece is well approached in a similar spirit of attentive mindfulness. If you are involved with Zen or yoga or some form of meditation, you will have practiced the act of simply paying attention; if this is an unaccustomed experience, Feldman provides an excellent entrée. A focused listener may notice patterns of sounds or may perceive small gradations when sounds are repeated (and therefore are not actually repeated at all). If you feel that you have lost the thread, don't panic. Simply start listening again, without worrying about anything beyond the momentary gesture, the immediacy of the sound of the moment. You may find as you listen that you are noticing moments in relation to each other. On the other hand, you may experience the piece as essentially still. Wrote Feldman in his 1981 essay *Crippled Symmetry*: 'Stasis, as it is utilized in painting, is not traditionally part of the apparatus of music. Music can achieve aspects of immobility, or the illusion of it: the Magritte-like world Satie evokes, of the "floating sculpture" of Varèse. The degree of stasis found in a Rothko or a Guston, were perhaps the most significant elements that I brought to my music from painting.'[56]

In fact the whole programme presented that day was a comment on emptiness, though the pre-programme talk named it 'departures'. A short a cappella piece by the Lithuanian composer Mindaugas Urbaitis, inspired by the 'Lacrimosa' of Mozart's *Requiem*, illustrated the technique that he calls 're-composition' or 'recycling'. Creating his own music around fragments of earlier composers, he is also creating in the context of the audience's memory, the result being a form of musical collage. This was followed by the Feldman *Rothko* piece for which the programme notes read like instructions for meditation practice.

This is for a contemplative piece in which sounds emerge from and fade into silence, celebrating paintings in which colour and form materialize almost imperceptibly from the background and darkness: in both the edges of sound and paint wisping out into transparency. The second half of the concert was the Mozart *Requiem*. The afternoon presented death and life: Mozart, Rothko and Feldman living on in their works.

Other composers demonstrate the importance of silence in their compositions, and most of these, interestingly, come from religious backgrounds and a meditative influence. From early on in the silence from which the pure sound floats out in the work of Hildegard of Bingen, through to contemporary works by Sofia Gubaidulina, Henryk Górecki, Veljo Tormis and Arvo Pärt, silence appears an integral part of the music. Others find a similar inspiration in natural space: John Luther Adams in Alaska, Per Nørgård in Denmark, Peter Sculthorpe in Australia, Peter Maxwell Davies in Orkney, R. Murray Schafer in Canada and Sigur Rós in Iceland immediately spring to mind. The extraordinary music of John Luther Adams expresses the place, time, weather and vast space of his home in Alaska. Rooted in place, attention and response to nature, it illustrates a considered move away from linearity, or horizontal time as he describes it, into vertical time, 'the presence of the moment'. This is a trajectory common to this journey of tracing echoes of emptiness throughout all the arts. Whether the origin of such music is internal or external, mind or land, silence and attention form twin pillars of this music along with the personal attention, practice and integrity of the composers – fruits of a philosophy of emptiness.

In the postmodern everything is possible – except for one single metanarrative. Thus in the current field of music practice it is as difficult to pick out a dominant narrative as it is within one piece. Possibilities are much more open; boundaries between genres and within individual works are constantly breached. But there are themes and trends, and these we have also seen in other fields.

Collage, for example, allows for reference to be made both vertically to the history of music, and horizontally, to different genres. Thus it can be a way of reassembling the deconstructed fragments, of embodying a kind of interdependence. Another major trend is that of improvisation. Interestingly, the teaching of improvisation relies on a kind of meditative or mindful teaching of 'deep listening' – listening without desire so as to be able to respond from an 'empty mind'. In the absence of rules, the artists themselves must train to become worthy instruments. What may seem an extreme of individualism travels paradoxically beyond the individual. Returning once more to John Cage, who at this point seems an ever more seminal figure in music practice:

> New art and music do not communicate an individual's conceptions in ordered structures, but they implement processes which are, as are our daily lives, opportunities for perception (observation and listening).[57]

### EMBODIED ART: DANCE

Contemporary dance demonstrates almost better than any other artistic discipline the blurring of the boundaries between forms. Partaking of music, movement and visual art, it presents a true contemporary interdisciplinary spectacle.

Meredith Monk is an exemplary contemporary artist whose practice spans the fields of dance and music, and exhibits so many of the traits that I have described. Influenced both by contemporary Western and Buddhist ideas, for decades she has been expressing her practice in works of both discipline and wild imagination.

I think about that 'empty' space a lot. That emptiness is what allows for something to actually evolve in a natural way. I've had to learn that over the years because one of the traps of being an artist is to always want to be creating, always wanting to produce.[58]

Akram Khan, a dancer initially trained in traditional Indian Kathak dance, has extended his range into contemporary dance, and in so doing has expanded the scope of the entire genre. Constantly pushing the boundaries of dance, he has collaborated with other artists from different genres, including Antony Gormley, Anish Kapoor, the classical ballerina Sylvie Guillem, the musician Nitin Sawhney, the actress Juliette Binoche and the National Ballet Company of China. Within such multiplicity, however, Khan is always aware of the space and emptiness from which forms emerge. Speaking of a work called *Kaash*, he noted:

It is important that we remind ourselves of the value of that which we cannot touch. Is it not true that the empty space inside the cup is what renders it useful? Similarly, the stillness between steps, the spaces between musical phrases and the empty spaces in space itself contain all the mysteries of their eventual forms.[59]

The title of another work, *Zero Degrees*, refers to the point where everything begins and everything ends. In the pieces Khan and his collaborator, the choreographer Sidi Larbi Cherkaoui, go on 'a journey to seek the reference point, the source, that "O" at life's core . . . this middle point through polar opposites; becoming/death, light/dark, chaos/order'. In another piece Cherkaoui collaborated with Antony Gormley and the monks from the Shaolin Temple of martial arts in China on a fantastic dance piece entitled *Sutra*. These collaborations embody the coming together of Eastern and Western ideas and genres within the field of contemporary dance. Cloud Gate Theatre of Taiwan is also notable in this arena for its exquisitely beautiful presentations that straddle oriental/occidental approaches, often using content from Eastern myths and movement from Chi Kung and martial arts set to Western music such as that of J. S. Bach and Arvo Pärt.

It is in the work of another choreographer, Wayne McGregor, that leading edge knowledge and technology strangely enter the domain of emptiness. Choreographing both for traditional companies such as the Royal Ballet and San Francisco Ballet, and his own contemporary company Wayne McGregor| Random Dance, the influence of a concern with unknowing is profoundly embedded throughout all aspects of his work; not merely referenced in the content, but deeply embodied in the way of creation. McGregor believes that 'dance works more in ambiguity and in discovery'. Personally, he has profoundly explored the ways of creativity and the often unconscious limitations of habitude. Working in conjunction with cognitive scientists he has explored the deep neuronal schema that programme our responses, those patterns and pre-existing filters which are engrained cognitively and through which we interpret the world while commonly being unaware of their existence. His exploration is in the service of freedom from habitude and in full awareness that how you shift attention affects the quality of an experience.

McGregor speaks of 'unknowing', 'undoing' and 'unlearning', and a recent work is entitled *Undance*. He has likened his exploration of computer-programmed tools, based on knowledge of mental and physical processes, to Cage's use of the I Ching to evade his own unconscious yet habitual choices in writing music. By creating a new and technologically founded language of movement and decision making based on insights from the mind sciences, he is exploring ways to help understand and enhance the dancers' imaginations. Through greater under-standing of kinaesthetic intelligence and the underlying schema of habit, McGregor is paradoxically attempting to evade habitual action. This is a paradox of seeking knowledge to evade habitual knowledge, of evading perceived necessity and acknowledging both contingency and our inbuilt defences against it, in order to elude false fixity and certainty and enhance creativity.

Technology comes to the aid of reflective attention. Meta-attention reveals the unconscious biases of everyday awareness. Thorough preparation paradoxically allows space for embodied response. Interestingly, *Undance* has been considered McGregor's most fluent and simple work to date. The fluency and flexibility of movement is joyful even when distorted or aggressive, embodying a quite amazing openness. Awareness become embodied.

* * *

We have seen that art, meditation and psychotherapy all foster and support a state of curious bare attention. Mark Epstein refers frequently to the psychoanalyst Donald Winnicott and his conception of that 'third space' that is neither inner nor outer, which he linked to play, creativity and spirituality, suggesting that this transitional space of bare attention, 'this capacity to know things as they are, qualified by mere existence, is what links the artist, the meditator and the psychotherapist'.[60] In the essay cited earlier concerning Anish Kapoor, Homi Bhabha also referred to this transitional space of Winnicott's in relation to Kapoor's revelation of emptiness through his work. It is within this space that we can tolerate unknowing, rest in the 'contrarium' – the term the artist and writer John Danvers uses to embrace the aim of those sceptics, mystics and artists who attempt to breach the gap between dualities and express the complementarity of either/or, neither/nor, particle and wave.[61]

Another psychologist, Christopher Bollas, writes of 'the aesthetic moment'. This involves a deep rapport in which self and object feel fused, 'reciprocally enhancing and mutually informative'.[62] Through exploration of this breaking of barriers between self and other, through deconstruction of the integrity of the object, and investigation of contingency, the 'agents of uncertainty', as Danvers names artists, delineate traces of emptiness throughout contemporary arts.

The journey through different art fields described above has, I hope, revealed the trace of a dialogue, a logic of complementarity as well as contrast, between sound and silence, listening and talking, mark and erasure, stasis and movement, artist and audience. Perhaps the poet Allen Ginsberg comes closest to expressing this when he says that the life of meditation and the life of art are both based on a similar conception of spontaneous mind; 'it means expanding the area of awareness, so that your awareness surrounds your thoughts, rather than that you enter into thoughts like a dream.'[63] Expanded awareness discovers and inhabits the emptiness around the myriad objects.

The artists noted all challenge the complacency of sound, the complacency of the visible, the complacency of substance. A philosophy of emptiness offers an alternative view that asks us to evade our habitual responses, the conventionally seen, heard and thought, and to look more closely, with more attention, below the surface, around and within substance, in the silence between sounds, to find an unconventional way of seeing reality – to see, hear and think afresh.

While the works shown in the exhibition 'Invisible', and many of the artists, writers and musicians I have mentioned, overtly emphasize emptiness as their subject and confound expectations of substance and presence, I have come to the thought that perhaps a more implicit understanding and expression of the demands of emptiness, of space and silence, is a necessary component of all great art. In a moving tribute at the time of the death of Seamus Heaney, Professor Roy Foster cited Heaney's lines referring to

> ... a space
> Utterly empty, utterly a source ...

He also told how in another work Heaney wrote of the absence of a tree as 'a kind of luminous emptiness'. It is this understanding of emptiness that is luminous and source that can transcend dichotomies of presence and absence, sound and silence.[64]

# EIGHT

# Empty Conclusions

And, nothing himself, beholds.
Nothing that is not there and the nothing that is.
Wallace Stevens, 'The Snow Man'

In the face of contingency, any neat conclusion is inappropriate and impossible, but I would like to revisit certain themes that have braided through this exploration of emptiness. We have followed a trail that has taken us from a fully formed philosophy of emptiness that is 2,500 years old and distant in space as well as time, and traced resonance and echoes creeping closer in both age and place to the present-day Western world. For many centuries in Western culture such echoes were faint, hardly heard at all, and emptiness generally had the meaning of loss, to be received with fear. As the certainties and grounds of Christian culture have been questioned and found wanting in the face of current science, society and experience, we have traced various contemporary Western resonances of emptiness. They are a response to a feeling of uncertainty and lack that engenders anguish. They are certainly not all bearing Eastern or Buddhist influence. Yet many point to ways – not of fear and evasion, but of doorways – through to a different, deeper understanding, of a *way* to live with contingency and evade the strictures and structures of certainty and orthodoxy. Because this experience of emptiness begins as a phenomenological response to the loss of authority it would be inappropriate, not to say pointless, for a philosophy of emptiness to be singular, unique and unmoving. It must be one of flexibility, of plurality. We can at best delineate the shape of the journey towards such a philosophy and the various themes that form its elements.

The journey towards a contemporary philosophy of emptiness etches a double movement. First there is a slipping away, a loss, in which the previous supports and authorities and beliefs are challenged and fall. The common psychological experience of emptiness frequently ends with this single movement and the emotional reaction to this feeling, which is to fill it. All around us we can see this movement towards distraction, consumption and dependence. A *philosophy* of emptiness, however, does not stop here, but continues to the second step. By resolving to pay attention to the feeling of lack and uncertainty, without being deceived by the diversion of blocking it, it discovers what is there in the emptiness: the reality, the process and potential that arises from the undistracted gaze.

As to the themes and tropes: first, a philosophy of emptiness must be close to *experience*; existential in that it is concerned with existence rather than essence, and embodied in that it is concerned with our embodied experience. Second, approaches to emptiness are *therapeutic*, signifying a way to deal with anguish, a path to living better. Third, a philosophy of emptiness is centred in *awareness* rather than evasion. Deep awareness of the construction of our experience, of the seduction of ego and permanence and possession, and of the bewitchment of language, leads to attempts to fully know the language we use and the way a 'self' develops, and causes us to understand language and self as empty of essence or inherent existence. Thus a further trope is that of *not-self*; explorations of emptiness have in common a deconstruction of the concept of an essential self in order to reveal its construction, to show it as process rather than essence, and to underline its *interdependence*. Another may be that of *ineffability*, or if not complete ineffability, of indefinability.

A final concern is that it is anti-dogmatic, *a central path*, always taking the middle way between presence and absence, always upsetting dualities. Its concern is with contingency, indeterminacy, lack of essence and of certainty; its philosophers are the agents of uncertainty. A philosophy of emptiness is against orthodoxy and totality, wary even of its own, teaching the emptiness of emptiness, for emptiness is quality rather than substance.

## EXPERIENCE

Throughout the preceding pages we have seen how experience lies at the centre of our concern. A philosophy of emptiness is a naturalistic philosophy concerned with the way we experience and live rather than with any external, transcendental presence that provides authority. It is a way, a path to well-being and to living in accordance with the best understanding of reality that we can achieve. It is a knowledge that must be realized in an embodied and emotional fashion, as well as intellectual one, in order that it may permeate all aspects of our lived experience. We can see how the first step of a philosophy of emptiness unfolds not just intellectually, but inevitably emotionally, through feelings of emptiness that may be experienced either with confusion or ultimately with clarity. The task is to face up to the inevitable contingency of life without being paralysed by fear or uncertainty, able to put one foot in front of another, travelling from step to step, day to day, open to both the lack of certainty and the freedom that an understanding of emptiness provides.

We have also seen how this intellectual, emotional and embodied understanding of emptiness threads throughout all aspects of life and knowledge, in particular in the oft-recurring alignment of philosophy, art and psychology. Perhaps Heidegger may stand as a supreme example of this, illustrated by his philosophy, his interpretation of poetic thought and his collaboration with the psychoanalyst Medard Boss, the founder of Daseinsanalyse. According to Boss, Heidegger had answered the first letter that Boss had ever sent to him in 1946, despite the amount of his correspondence and the fact that Boss was unknown to him, because

> he had hoped that through me – a physician and a psychiatrist – his thinking would escape the confines of the philosopher's study and become of benefit to wide circles in particular to a large number of suffering human beings.[1]

The areas of philosophy that have occurred here are those most concerned with practice, from the natural understanding of Taoism, through the early psychology of Buddhist thought, through Hellenistic philosophies concerned with paths to well-being, eudaemonia and ataraxia, with a largely God-filled gap, until modern times and the breaking up of such widely held beliefs brought thinkers back to their phenomenological experience of contingency.

For centuries in the Western tradition, theory and practice were separated: intellectual explorations of philosophy, even psychology, were unlinked from the implications of their embodied lived practice; rationality and theory took prime position over emotion and action. Recent trends have seen this priority questioned and even overturned (often, alas, to an extreme extent, a rebalancing that merely moves from one end of the spectrum to the other, resulting in an equal if opposite imbalance). As noticed in a recent book:

> The concept of practice is oddly underdeveloped within the Western philosophical tradition, despite being

central to the major modern ruptures of that tradition which form the corpus of critical theory and the artistic avant-garde.[2]

In this strange but telling study of copying, Marcus Boon investigates contemporary commercial and artistic culture in a manner deeply informed by an understanding of non-duality and emptiness as lack of essence. He concludes the book with a recommendation for a reinvigorated, critical concept of practice in cultural and political theory.

Within the field of the arts we have seen how a concern with artistic practice itself, a practice that often now includes the viewer, has come into focus. However, while all the domains that we have explored above in the light of emptiness display at least a theoretical understanding of emptiness and interdependence, a concern with process rather than product, and an understanding of the fluidity and construction of what once appeared solid and permanent, folk psychology, the common-sense understanding rooted in our emotional reaction to these changes, has lagged behind. Thus this return to practice holds within it a concern that is therapeutic.

### THERAPEUTIC AIM

A philosophy of emptiness is proposed for a reason, as an antidote to misunderstanding. Deconstruction of our natural and cultural constructions has as its aim that second step towards a *philosophy* of emptiness, the revelation of reality, with the implication, explicit or implicit, that we shall live better, more happily, more compassionately, with this understanding.

All the philosophies of emptiness that we have explored have a therapeutic aim. The four truths of the Buddha present analysis, all life entails suffering; diagnosis, the cause is ignorance and desire; prognosis, liberation is possible; and prescription, the eightfold path. The early Greek schools of thought surveyed above were all concerned with eudaemonia (well-being), and with ways of understanding and detachment that may help us to achieve quietude. Following Hadot ('First and foremost, philosophy presented itself as a therapeutic, intended to cure mankind's anguish'[3]), we have seen how these philosophies represented forms of life defined by ideals of wisdom whose purpose was therapeutic. During the many centuries of the hegemony of Christian belief, emptiness (with the exception of certain mystical writers) was considered only as lack, and in the contemporary era, where we find its marks after so many centuries of neglect, the trail has often been marked by description rather than prescription. However, it is possible to see a line of therapeutically intended practice from the mindfulness and meditation of Buddhism through prayer and contemplation to today's psychotherapies. As Heidegger's work was foundational for the psychoanalyst Medard Boss in his practice of therapy, so Buddhist philosophy and practice have directly inspired and influenced several other strands of psychotherapy. Most markedly this is shown in the ever-increasing current interest in mindfulness, abstracted from any religious or historical background, for the relief of stress, chronic pain and depression.

In an often-repeated simile, the Buddha likened the dharma to a raft that should be set down once the river has been crossed. Wittgenstein spoke of his work as an attempt to release the fly from the fly bottle, as a therapy of language. Like Wittgenstein's work, that of Lakoff and Johnson to unravel the metaphors we live by aims to reattach language to the embodied experience from which it sprung and to bring life back to dead metaphors now taken literally. One of our most fundamental metaphors is that of reality as substance. The Buddhist philosophy of emptiness and its subsequent path leads to replacement of this root metaphor with that of reality as empty of essence, and a continuous realization of language itself as metaphoric and shifting rather than representative, thus dismantling the reifying tendency of language. In a less obviously argued fashion this is also what much contemporary art attempts to show. Behind these trends in both psychotherapy and art lies the resource of centuries of practices of attention.

## AWARENESS

We have seen experience of contemplative reflection advocated by many disciplines. All propose awareness rather than evasion: awareness of the processes of life, of the processes of the mind, of the bewitchment of language, the seduction of ego and the search for certainty. They suggest ways and practices of awareness to help us see that we may have some choice in our actions and beliefs rather than being the victims of unconsidered reactions. With careful attention we may consider fully the language we use and understand the way ego develops, that we may understand language and ego as empty of inherent essence. What remains from such deconstruction is not the emptiness of privation, but the foundational emptiness, interdependence, contingency and unknowability of the world and the ongoing process of selfing. Knowing and inhabiting this, we may be enabled to live better, more happily, day by day, step by step, for ourselves and for others. Attention is at the heart of consciousness, agency and selfing. In the words of a philosopher of mind: 'attention is a finite commodity, and it is absolutely essential to living a good life'.[4] It should thus be seen as a precious resource for good education, that through neuroplasticity, good habits of attention may be instilled at an early age to counter the almost toxic levels of attention deficit, stress and anxiety that much of our current entertainment and advertising media encourage. Moreover, a non-egoic awareness may bring us alive to the richness of the world, if we can shift our addiction to self.

Not-self has been an important topic throughout this discussion, a conception of not-self that refers not to the non-existence of *some* conception of self, but to the loss of the understanding of self as an independent, permanent and partless entity, and a reconsideration of selfing as a process, a construction, a designation, even a task. One of the earliest Western expressions of this understanding comes from someone I have not yet mentioned in these pages, but whose influence pervades them: Michel de Montaigne. Deeply influenced by Sceptical and Hellenistic writers, Montaigne undertook the first interior exploration of experience. Unsurprisingly, he found the heterogeneity of the self.

> We are all patchwork, and of such an unformed and diverse composition that each part, each moment, plays its role. And one finds as much difference between us and ourselves, as between us and others.[5]

Here I would like to point to some of the implications of this on both an individual level and that of humanity. For the individual we see that not-self does not mean extinction, but more in the light of Keats's negative capability, 'that is when a man is capable of being in uncertainties, mysteries, doubts, without any irritable reaching after fact or reason'.[6] If one can be free of 'self' and its egocentric imperatives, then one may be open to world, to unknowing and possibility, a possibility that is the very lifeblood of the good artist and the compassionate soul. A true understanding of not-self, rather than obliterating the self, actually provides it with a support that is entirely lacking for the isolated, independent essential self, separated from all 'other'. For the isolated and rigid self, emptiness can only be experienced as loss and lack, evoking the reaction of compulsive filling with consumption and distraction. For the self that understands its implication in the web of life, emptiness of self equates with resilience and with *interdependence*. As the other face of emptiness is that of suchness, so the other face of non-self from the alienated and needy one described above is its interdependence with other, as David Loy describes in Buddhist terms:

> if each link of dependent origination is conditioned by all the others, then to become completely groundless is also to become completely grounded, not in some particular, but in the whole network of interdependent relations that constitute the world. The supreme irony of my struggle to ground myself is that it cannot succeed because I am already grounded *in the totality*.[7]

Perhaps the most profound Buddhist expression of this comes from the twelfth-century Japanese writer Dōgen:

> Practice that confirms things by taking the self to them is illusion: for things to come forward and practice and confirm the self is enlightenment ... To learn the Buddha Way is to learn one's self. To learn one's self is to forget one's self. To forget one's self is to be confirmed by all dharmas [phenomena].[8]

It is this same understanding that Thomas Merton expresses when, having been reading Nishida Kitaro's *Study of Good*, he writes in his journal: 'To be open to the nothingness which I am is to grasp the all in whom I am.'[9] As Einstein beautifully described it in 1921:

> A human being is part of a whole, called by us the Universe, a part limited in time and space. He experiences

himself, his thoughts and feelings as something separated from the rest, a kind of optical delusion of his consciousness. This delusion is a kind of prison for us, restricting us to a few persons nearest us. Our task must be to free ourselves from this prison by widening our circles of compassion to embrace all living creatures and the whole of nature in its beauty.[10]

This sentiment appears throughout the works often cited here. The Buddhist philosopher Santideva said:

In the same way as the hands and so forth
Are regarded as the limbs of the body,
Likewise why are embodied creatures
Not regarded as limbs of life.[11]

We might compare this to the statement of Marcus Aurelius that 'we must love other people with all our hearts for rational beings are not only parts of the same whole, but the limbs of the same body.'[12]

### INEFFABILITY

All of the above themes have grappled with the fundamental difficulty of expression. To express them, philosophers, scientists and artists have frequently made use of neologisms and negations in order to evade any restrictive definition. For while grounded in individual experience they all point to process that is upstream of all classification, category and language. The awareness and attention described above is the condition of possibility enabling the expression of emptiness, the experience of which is prior to articulation. We have seen the difficulty that Meister Eckhart, Dōgen and Heidegger experienced in trying to put their concepts into words, the ways in which they had to twist conventional speech in order to surpass convention and torture language to express what comes before language. It is said that Aristotle complained of the unorthodox word order used by Heraclitus. The methods, and indeed sometimes the message, of much of contemporary art are initially shocking. The intention is to cleanse the lenses through which we see the world, or perhaps better said, to draw attention to lenses that are transparent and unnoticed but which have a profound and limiting effect on the way we experience the world. Beyond language we also have seen the way Wayne McGregor is using computerized 'choreographic thinking tools' to achieve a similar result with movement. We may in time find that this is the equivalent to the way out of the Ego Tunnel, or the rotation from the egocentric to the allocentric processes of consciousness.

## A CENTRAL PATH

Most importantly, a philosophy of emptiness that understands contingency and impermanence must remain constantly aware of the endless tendency to reify and identify, and must never refuse to shift its gaze reflexively to itself. Every groundbreaking discovery may become the new orthodoxy. The delicate balance of the middle way is a tightrope; a knife's edge between is and is not, between positive and negative, realism and nihilism. Thus philosophers of emptiness must look to their footwork as dancers in space and language.

\* \* \*

I began this writing from the theoretical perspective of a grounding in Buddhist thought and the experiential one of working as a psychotherapist. Exploring the wider resonances, the idea of emptiness has become more and more replaced in my thinking by the idea of *openness*; that is openness to contingency and a challenge to all philosophies of essence, foundation and being. Many days spent writing in California in a hillside garden that on winter mornings looked out into nothing but mist, giving the feeling of living within a Chinese ink painting, provided me with an apposite image. The process of emptiness and the fullness of interdependence is complicated, more a misty intertwining than an either/or.

A philosophy of emptiness should provide an acceptance of contingency, and a way to live with uncertainty, similar perhaps to Keats's negative capability, a way to live an engaged and meaningful life despite or rather *within* unknowing; a way that avoids the seductions of certainty. Yet within uncertainty we need some guidelines even as we speak of the end of metanarratives. As I was coming to the end of writing this book, in a dialogue between two philosophers concerning *The Future of Religion*, I came across this:

> There are no facts only interpretations . . . the end of the metanarratives is not the unveiling of a 'true' state of affairs in which the metanarratives 'no longer are'; it is, on the contrary, a process which, given that we are fully immersed in it and cannot regard it from outside, we are called upon to grasp a guiding thread that we can use in order to project its further development; that is to remain inside it as interpreters rather than as objective recorders of facts.[13]

I see emptiness as that guiding thread that may helpfully keep us from closure yet steer us through indeterminacy on the middle path between is and is not, in the understanding that experience, existence and language are all thoroughly relational, plural and interconnected.

If the concept of emptiness appeared initially alien to Western sensibility, perhaps now we can acknowledge the value of this strangeness as a new lens through which to see things afresh. Emptiness has nothing to do with nothing. Paradoxically, emptiness, rather than being negative, may act as an antidote to loss of ultimate foundations if it is considered, as presented in early philosophies, together with its belief in inter-dependence. Stephen Batchelor has perhaps expressed it most neatly, speaking of 'the emptiness of necessity and the embrace of contingency'.[14] The definition of contingency is: depending on something else. Happening by chance. Tathata, suchness. The infinite movement of things, the way the world worlds. Existence and experience. Spinoza wrote:

> It is of the nature of reason to regard things not as con-tingent, but as necessary. It perceives this necessity of things truly, that is, as it is in itself. But necessity of things is the necessity itself of the eternal nature of God. There-fore it is the nature of reason to regard things under this species of eternity.[15]

Even for Spinoza, defence against contingency necessitated reason, radical objectivity and God (even if his definition of God was unacceptable to his peers). Indeed, most religions, and indeed much of philosophy, have been predicated on such defence and such necessity. Until quite recent times, Buddhist and Taoist thought alone, along perhaps with Hellenistic philosophies possibly influenced by the former, appeared able to embrace contingency and to treat the necessity for eternal essence, or Truth or God, as suspect. It seems to me that at the end of the trail, a philosophy of emptiness is a philosophy of such suspicion. As a guiding thread to living rather than philosophy, theory or religious truth, rather than meeting contingency with theoretical necessity, it brings us back to life as it is lived; to experience freed from essence and definition; to a clear-sighted openness to experience lived with attention.

For the logical definition of contingency is that which is neither logically necessary nor logically impossible, so that its truth or falsity can be established only by sensory observation. Post-theism and post-theory, the thread of emptiness can open up a way to live without loss of meaning along with loss of foundation.

Thus the fundamental distinction between philosophies of emptiness and philosophies of presence, one that overlaps with a major distinction between Eastern and Western ways of thinking that affects all aspects of culture, is that the former understand a fundamental and inseparable connection between emptiness and presence, substance and space, which in Western philosophic history have been considered antagonistic.

> To be empty is not to be non-existent; rather, to exist is to be empty. Emptiness is not an alternative to reality, it is the only kind of reality that anything can have.[16]

This has two important corollaries. As a result, first, every phenomenon becomes more contingent and less definable in its own essential individual identity, dependent on its context and interrelationship; yet, second, this loss of essence and gain of contingency does not imply non-existence, lack of value or resultant nihilism, for the interdependent phenomena are connected with, by and through their emptiness. Many aspects of Western postmodern thought can be seen to understand interconnectedness while missing the deep correlation to emptiness, leaving phenomena in a surface network of style without meaning.

At the end of this journey I hope that we have taken both steps of the journey and see emptiness without fear – not as lack, but rather as the ultimate impossibility of certainty and totality. Emptiness stands not as any thing or presence or guarantee; it stands for the way the process processes, offering us a very different approach from our traditional one of dualities; presence/absence, substance/mind and so forth. Rather than totality or transcendence we may find confirmation in the web of immanent relationships, a kind of immanent transcendence that is horizontal rather than vertical: that is, dynamic, changeful and compassionate. Rather than coming from some guarantor of authority that stands outside the system, our confidence comes from implication in the whole network, from uncertainty and from contingency itself. Moreover, practices of attention may affirm the contingent, lived world and its unknowability in a new way, thus going beyond the idea of emptiness as lack towards enriching our experience. The task of facing emptiness is to question and unlearn the beliefs that we take for granted, the invisible lenses through which we habitually view the world that are embedded in our language and may be, thinking of the Ego Tunnel, instantiated in our brains.

Throughout many books George Steiner has grieved that we have lost real presences and expressed nostalgia for the absolute, believing that it is the 'God question' that has fuelled much of the great art and that a hunger for the transcendent, the supernatural, informs human sensibility. He has lamented that in the light of deconstruction, we now have nothing beyond appearance. Yet in a recent work, on the books he has never written, he admits that what he has come to believe 'with compelling intensity is the absence of God' and that 'The emptiness I feel has enormous power . . . It is a nihilism brimful with the unknown.'[17] While appreciating the power and the unknown of emptiness, I would question in their light the contention that it is a nihilism as generally understood. It is indeed nihilism in the sense of the viewpoint that traditional values and beliefs are objectively unfounded, but it is free of the (emotional?) corollary that life therefore is futile and meaningless. I would counter with the question of why we need anything more. We have the immediacy of experience: in the present and in the infinite breadth (not the totality), the Sublime is *now*. Yet there is indeed a sense that if all we have is the experience, and it is limited to *my* experience, then we are left merely with objects and consumption – and then the desert becomes a lack that must be filled, becomes a Las Vegas. As Mark Epstein pointed out:

> Buddhism is important to art at this moment because it both speaks to and serves as an antidote for the self-conscious nihilism that has become so prominent in our deconstructivist ideologies . . . Far from the ironic bravado and barely concealed shock that inform much of the postmodern response to the breakdown of the art object and the self, Buddhism offers a gentle and penetrating wisdom that accepts the insubstantial nature of this world without denigrating it. Through its doctrine of emptiness Buddhism affirms the primacy of the potential space in which the creative act occurs.[18]

For these reasons Buddhist philosophy, a secular Buddhism and the influence of David Brook's 'neural Buddhists' are becoming indeed both evermore widespread and helpful in mainstream culture. Yet it is not only Buddhists who understand emptiness, as I hope the preceding pages have shown. Two contemporary American writers, one a Christian, one from a Mormon background, express a sense of emptiness, without fear and as possibility, as well as anyone has over the centuries, and I would like to end with their cries of hope. First, Annie Dillard brings together the themes of interdependence and attention so finely:

> The death of the self of which the great writers speak is no violent act. It is merely the joining of the great rock heart of the earth in its roll. It is merely the slow cessation of the will's spirits and the intellect's chatter: it is waiting

like a hollow bell with stilled tongue. *Fuge, tace, quiesce.*
The waiting is the thing.[19]

And from Terry Tempest Williams, on seeing the photograph
*Earthrise*, taken from the moon:

> If in fact we are in free fall, we can relax, because we also
> know there is no ground, so no need for a parachute. If
> we are a part of the whole, what more do we want.[20]

From considering emptiness as lack of being, we may see that
ultimately emptiness is not empty of being, but is rather the
space at the centre of the jug, and that considered thus, it is
emptiness that restores being and potential to phenomena in
all its conventional existence and all of its mystery.

Finally, bearing Nagarjuna's warning, ringing down through
the years, that

> Buddhas say emptiness
> Is relinquishing opinions.
> Believers in emptiness
> Are incurable.[21]

Let us return to Tsongkhapa's statement that emptiness rather
than a belief is the path on which the centred person moves,
and at this point speak not of a philosophy of emptiness but
rather of a *way* or *orientation*. Emptiness, following the tracks
both of ancient sages and contemporary scientists and artists,
may provide an alternative view for Westerners long trapped
in philosophies of presence and substance, a middle path
between is and is not, eternalism and nihilism, sound and
silence, stasis and movement, talking and listening, mark and
erasure, all linked in a logic of reciprocity, of complementarity
rather than competition.

Looking backwards to our journey along Gary Snyder's trails in the High Sierra of California, Heidegger's woodpaths through the Black Forest, the ever-flowing river path of Heraclitus, and the many roads of contemporary art and science, let us end with Nagarjuna, the singer of emptiness, to inspire our own ongoing paths:

When emptiness is possible
Everything is possible;
Were emptiness impossible,
Nothing would be possible.[22]

# REFERENCES

## INTRODUCTION

1 B. Kosko, *Fuzzy Thinking* (London, 1994).
2 M. Soeng, *The Heart of the Universe* (Somerville, MA, 2010), p. 35.
3 'Momentariness', 'transitoriness' and 'now' all come from M. Soeng, *Heart*, pp. 42, 45. 'Relativity' was used by T. Stcherbatsky in his *Conception of Buddhist Nirvana*. In the appendix, in which he translates chapters of Candrakirti's *Prasannapada*, he translates the term *sunyata* as relativity.
4 From an interview of 1974 excerpted in Kostelanetz, *Conversing with Cage* (New York, 1988), p. 70, and cited in J. Baas, *Smile of the Buddha* (Berkeley, CA, 2005), p. 170.
5 Ibid., p. 171.
6 K. Larson, *Where the Heart Beats* (New York, 2012), pp. 275–7, quoting from R. Fleming and W. Duckworth, eds, *John Cage at Seventy-five* (Cranbury, NJ, 1989), pp. 21, 22.

## ONE: EXPERIENCE

1 This is S. Batchelor's translation in *Buddhism Without Beliefs* (New York, 1997), p. 75, of Tsongkhapa's *rtsa she tik chen rigs pa'i rgya mtsho* (Sarnath, 1973). This work is a commentary to Nagarjuna's second-century text *Mulamadhyamakakarika*.
2 E. Thomas, *The South Country* [1909] (Stanbridge, Dorset, 2009), p. 231.
3 L. Govinda, *Creative Meditation* (London, 1977), p. 36.
4 G. Snyder, 'Introduction' to *Beneath a Single Buddhist Moon*, ed. K. Johnson and C. Paulenich (Boston, MA, 1991), p. 1.

5  Ibid., p. 2.

6  M. Oliver, *A Lesson from James Wright in Evidence* (Tarsett, Northumberland, 2009).

7  P. Hadot, *Philosophy as a Way of Life* (Oxford, 1995), p. 271.

8  Ibid., p. 84.

9  G. Snyder, *The Poetics of Emptiness* (Kensington, CA, 1989), p. 25.

10  M. Abrimović, in *Buddhism in Contemporary Art,* ed. J. Baas and M. J. Jacobs (Berkeley, CA, 2004), p. 188.

11  R. Davidson and S. Begley, *The Emotional Life of Your Brain* (New York, 2012). See especially chap. 11 for ways to change your emotional patterns.

12  J. H. Austin, *Selfless Insight* (Boston, MA, 2009), p. 219.

## TWO: THE BUDDHIST PHILOSOPHY OF *SUNYATA*

1  Since this is not an academic work, all Sanskrit and Pali terms are without diacriticals. I have used Pali terms in relation to Early Buddhism, which is presented in this language; elsewhere I have used Sanskrit.

2  *Dhammapada*, trans. T. Byrom (London, 1976), p. 3.

3  Bhikkhu Nanamoli and Bhikkhu Bodhi, trans, *The Middle Length Discourses of the Buddha* (Boston, MA, 1995), p. 283.

4  Dalai Lama, *The Meaning of Life From a Buddhist Perspective* (Boston, MA, 1992), p. 5.

5  Nanamoli and Bodhi, *Middle Length Discourses,* p. 655.

6  Ibid., p. 355.

7  For a fine description of these matters, see S. Hamilton, *Identity and Experience* (London, 1996), especially p. 130.

8  Namamoli and Bodhi, *Middle Length Discourses*, p. 83.

9  Ibid., pp. 965–78.

10  Bhikkhu Bodhi, *Connected Discourses of the Buddha* (Boston, MA, 2000), p. 163.

11  Kenneth Inada, trans., *Nagarjuna: A Translation of His Mulamadhyamakakarika* (Tokyo, 1970), p. 39.

12  Ibid.

13  S. Batchelor, *Verses from the Center* (New York, 2000), p. 124.

14  Thich Nuat Hanh, *Heart of Understanding* (Berkeley, CA, 1988), p. 3.
15  Batchelor, *Verses*, p. 124.
16  Ibid., p. 129.
17  Ibid., p. 22.
18  Samyutta Nikaya, 12.15, trans. S. Batchelor (personal communication).
19  Nagarjuna, *Mulamadhyamakakarika*, trans. S. Batchelor (personal communication).
20  S. Batchelor (personal communication). Interestingly this brings together the four truths or tasks of Early Buddhism, the teaching of Nagarjuna of the second century and that of Tsongkhapa in the fourteenth century.
21  K. Dowman, *The Flight of the Garuda* (London, 1994), p. 88.
22  J. Garfield, 'Study and Practice with Nagarjuna's Dharma', from BCBS *Insight Journal*, 13 September 2011, www.dharma.org/bacbs.
23  Batchelor, *Verses*, p. 123.

THREE: FOLLOWING THE TAO

1   C. Thubron, *The Silk Road* (London, 2006), p. 45.
2   Lao Tseu, *Tao Te king*, trans. Marcel Conche (Paris, 2003), p. 33.
3   Lao Tsu, *Tao Te Ching*, trans Gia-Fu Feng and J. English (London, 1973), verse 2.
4   A. Waley, *The Way and Its Power* (London, 1934), verse 40.
5   Lao Tsu, *Tao Te Ching*, verse 14.
6   Ibid., verse 40.
7   F. Jullien, *Vital Nourishment* (New York, 2007), trans. Arthur Goldhammer, p. 140.
8   Waley, *The Way and Its Power*, p. 53.
9   F. Jullien, *The Great Image Has No Form; or, On the Nonobject through Painting* (Chicago, IL, 2009), p. 5.
10  Ibid., p. 20.
11  Ibid., p. 79.
12  Jullien, *Vital Nourishment*, p. 140. Throughout this section

I am most indebted to Jullien's extraordinary interpretations of Chinese thought.

13 Waley, *The Way and Its Power*, verse 22.

14 B. Watson, trans., *The Complete Works of Chuang Tzu* (New York, 1968), p. 143.

15 Ibid., p. 132.

16 Ibid., p. 58.

17 Ibid., p. 97.

18 Ibid., p. 143.

19 Ibid., p. 5.

20 J. Humphries, *Reading Emptiness* (Albany, NY, 1999), p. 6.

21 Jullien, *The Great Image*, p. 46.

22 Ibid., p. 113.

23 F. Jullien, *In Praise of Blandness*, trans. Paula M. Varsano (Cambridge, MA, 2007), especially pp. 116, 133, 118.

24 L. Joon, *Void: Mapping the Invisible in Korean Art* (Seoul, 2007), n.p. An extract from this appears in S. Morley, ed., *The Sublime* (London, 2010), p. 102.

25 Jullien, *The Great Image*, p. 181.

26 Ibid., p. 216.

27 Conche, *Tao Te king*, p. 34.

## FOUR: MOVING WESTWARDS

1 S. Batchelor, *Confessions of a Buddhist Atheist* (New York, 2010), p. 117.

2 Fragment 10 from *Heraclitus: Fragments*, trans. and ed. T. M. Robinson (Toronto, 1987). Subsequent translations of Heraclitus are from this source.

3 Ibid., Fragment 49a; fragment 67.

4 Fragment 65, cited in T. McEvilley, *The Shape of Ancient Thought* (New York, 2002), p. 38.

5 A. Kuzminski, *Pyrrhonism* (Lanham, MD, 2008), p. 31.

6 C. W. Huntington, *The Emptiness of Emptiness* (Honolulu, HI, 1989), p. 160.

7 Kuzminski, *Pyrrhonism*, p. 58.

8 This is particularly interesting to remember because in a

future chapter we look at some contemporary neuroscientific views of the way our brains form our reality, what Thomas Metzinger calls 'the Ego Tunnel'. See chapter Six.

9  Kuzminski, *Pyrrhonism*, p. 141.
10 M. Conche, *Pyrrhon ou l'apparence* (Paris, 1994), p. 152. Conche is quoting from F. Nietzsche, *Oeuvres philosophiques complètes*, XIV (Paris, 1977), p. 127. I am extremely grateful to Stephen Batchelor for introducing me to Conche, for much consequent discussion and for his translations.
11 Conche, *Pyrrhon*, p. 111; translations by S. Batchelor based on those of Conche, and D. N. Sedley and A. A. Long, *The Hellenistic Philosophers* (Cambridge, 1987), p. 15.
12 Ibid., p. 60 (trans. S. Batchelor).
13 Ibid., p. 222 (my translation).
14 Sutta Nipata 802. 2. Atthakavagga, 3. Paramatthaka Sutta, trans. Thanissaro Bhikkhu, at www.ripassana.com.
15 Cited by McEvilley, *Shape of Ancient Thought*, p. 495.
16 Ibid., p. 458.
17 Ibid., p. 370.
18 Ibid., p. 611
19 P. Hadot, *Philosophy as a Way of Life*, trans. Arnold Davidson (Oxford, 1995), p. 59.
20 Ibid., p. 83.

FIVE: PHILOSOPHIC MODERNITY

1 M. A. Sells, *Mystical Languages of Unsaying* (Chicago, IL, 1994), p. 4.
2 Johannis Scotti Eriugenae, *Periphyseon (De Divisione Naturae)*, ed. and trans. I. P. Sheldon-Williams and L. Bieler (Dublin, 1972), 3.60, cited by Sells, *Mystical Languages*, p. 45.
3 From Meister Eckhart, *Selected Treatises and Sermons*, trans. J. Clark and J. Skinner (London, 1958), and cited in D. O'Neal, ed., *Meister Eckhart, from Whom God Hid Nothing* (Boston, MA, 1996), p. 119.
4 J. Derrida, 'How to Avoid Speaking, Denials', in S. Budick

and W. Iser, *Languages of the Unsayable* (Stanford, CA, 1987), pp. 30–70.

5   M. Fox, *Breakthrough* (New York, 1980), p. 215. These and the following quotations come from Sermon 15 and were chosen since they illustrated in one place many of the tropes for which Meister Eckhart is best known and which also resonate with ideas of emptiness.

6   Ibid., pp. 214–15.

7   These discontinuous lines come from St John of the Cross, *Verses Written on an Ecstasy of Complete Contemplation* (my translation).

8   These discontinuous lines comes from *The Ascent of Mount Carmel* (my translation).

9   H. Silverman, ed., *Philosophy and Non Philosophy since Merleau Ponty* (London, 1988), p. 1.

10  K. Jaspers, cited in T. Merton, *Dancing in the Water of Life* (San Francisco, CA, 1997), p. 68.

11  Ibid., p. 190.

12  The first quotation comes from L. Wittgenstein, *Tractatus Logico-Philosophicus*, trans D. Pear and B. McGuiness (London, 1969), p. 151. The second comes from L. Wittgenstein, *Prototractatus* (London, 1971), pp. 15–16.

13  L. Wittgenstein, *On Certainty*, cited in H. Dreyfus, *Being-in-the-World* (Cambridge, MS, 1991), p. 155.

14  Dreyfus, *Being-in-the-World*, p. 25.

15  M. Heidegger, *The End of Philosophy and the Task of Thinking*, trans. J. Stambaugh in *Basic Writings*, ed. D. F. Krell (New York, 1977), cited by J. Sallis, 'Echoes: Philosophy and Non-philosophy After Heidegger', in Silverman, *Philosophy and Non-Philosophy*, p. 95.

16  This was stated in a reading given as part of the 2011 Dartington International Summer School of Music, 15 August 2011.

17  See R. May, *Heidegger's Hidden Sources* (London, 1996); G. Parkes, ed., *Heidegger and Asian Thought* (Honolulu, HI, 1987); J. Stambaugh, *Thoughts on Heidegger* (Washington, DC, 1991).

18  M. Heidegger, *On the Way to Language* (San Francisco, CA, 1971), p. 19.

19  M. Heidegger, *Country Path Conversations* (Bloomington, IN, 2010), pp. 84–5.

20  Ibid., p. 87.

21  Ibid., pp. 80, 92.

22  Ibid.

23  Heidegger, *On the Way to Language,* pp. 18, 19.

24  Heidegger, *Country Path Conversations,* p. 78.

25  M. Heidegger, *The End,* cited by Sallis, 'Echoes', in Silverman, *Philosophy and Non-Philosophy*, p. 101.

26  Nishitani Keiji, *Religion and Nothingness* (Berkeley, CA, 1982), p. 47.

27  Ibid., p. 105.

28  Ibid., p. 111.

29  M. Heidegger, *What is Called Thinking?* (New York, 1968), p. 78.

30  A. Klein, *Meeting the Great Bliss Queen* (Boston, MA, 1995), p. 137.

31  J. Derrida, *Margins of Philosophy* (Chicago, IL, 1982), p. 21.

32  See D. Loy, *NonDuality* (New Haven, CT, 1988); R. Magliola, *Derrida on the Mend* (West Lafayette, IN, 1984); H. Coward and T. Fosshay, eds, *Derrida and Indian Philosophy* (Albany, NY, 1992).

33  M. Robinson, *Absence of Mind* (New Haven, CT, 2010), pp. 34–5.

34  M. Merleau-Ponty, *The Phenomenology of Perception* (London, 1986), p. xx.

35  G. Lakoff and M. Johnson, *Metaphors We Live By* (Chicago, IL, 1980) and *Philosophy in the Flesh* (New York, 1999); and M. Johnson, *The Body in the Mind* (Chicago, IL, 1987), *Moral Imagination* (Chicago, IL, 1993) and *The Meaning of the Body* (Chicago, IL, 2007).

36  C. Huntingdon, 'The System of the Two Truths in the Prasannapadā and the Madyamakāvatāra', *Journal of Indian Philosophy*, XI (1983), pp. 77–106.

37  M. Blanchot, *The Infinite Conversation* (Minneapolis, MN, 1993), pp. 299, 300.

38  R. Barthes, *The Neutral* (New York, 2005), pp. 6, 7, 10, 45.
39  H. Lawson, *Closure* (London, 2001), p. 4.
40  Q. Meillassoux, *After Finitude* (London, 2008).


SIX: SCIENTIFIC INDETERMINISM

1  Lucretius, *The Nature of Things*, trans. A. E. Stallings
   (London, 2007), p. 13.
2  L. M. Krause, 'The Godless Particle', *Newsweek,* 9 July 2012.
3  Recent experiments have apparently questioned the limitation
   of the speed of light. Whether these experiments will be
   corroborated remains to be seen.
4  R. Lea, in a review of R. Panek, *The 4% Universe: Dark Matter,
   Dark Energy, and the Race to Discover the Rest of Reality*
   (London, 2011), in Saturday *Guardian*, 18 March 2011.
5  W. L. Ames, 'Emptiness and Quantum Theory', in *Buddhism
   and Science*, ed. B. A. Wallace (New York, 2003), p. 295. I am
   indebted to William Ames for his clear exposition here that is
   comprehensible to a non-scientist.
6  This comes from the BBC television programme *The Wonders
   of the Universe,* presented by Professor B. Cox, BBC Four,
   28 January 2012.
7  Mu Soeng, *The Heart of the Universe* (Somerville, MS, 2010),
   p. 36.
8  A. Naess, 'The Shallow and the Deep', *Inquiry*, XVI (1973),
   p. 98, cited in *Nature in Asian Traditions of Thought*,
   ed. J. B. Callicott and R. Ames (Albany, NY, 1989), p. 59.
9  Ibid., p. 31.
10  A. Zajonc, ed., *The New Physics and Cosmology: Dialogues
    with the Dalai Lama* (Oxford, 2003), p. 37.
11  Ibid., p. 48.
12  P. Broks, *Into the Silent Land* (London, 2003), p. 41.
13  D. Dennett, *Consciousness Explained* (London, 1993), p. 42;
    M. Gazzaniga, *The Ethical Brain* (New York, 2005), p. 147.
14  C. Taylor, *Sources of the Self* (Cambridge, MA, 1989), p. 514.
15  W. James, *Principles of Psychology* (Cambridge, MA, 1981), p. 290.
16  C. Geertz, *Available Light* (Princeton, NJ, 2000), p. 205.

17  G. Strawson, 'Self and SESMET', *Journal of Consciousness Studies*, VI/4 (1999), pp. 99–135.

18  T. Metzinger, *The Ego Tunnel* (New York, 2009), p. 35.

19  Ibid., p. 38.

20  See S. Gebhart, *Why Love Matters* (London, 2004), for the story of this. Also the works of Alan Schore and Daniel Siegel.

21  R. Davidson and S. Begley, *The Emotional Life of Your Brain* (London, 2012); R. Hanson, *Buddha's Brain* (Oakland, CA, 2009).

22  For a discussion of this see Gay Watson, *Resonance of Emptiness* (London, 1998), chap. 1.

23  See www.mind/lifeinstitute.org.

24  David Brooks, 'Opinion', *The New York Times*, 13 May 2008.

25  Metzinger, *The Ego Tunnel*, p. 235.

26  James, *Principles*, p. 401.

27  I. McGilchrist, *The Master and the Emissary* (New Haven, CT, 2009), p. 4.

28  Ibid., p. 93.

29  Ibid., p. 277.

30  Ibid., p. 97.

SEVEN: ARTISTIC EMPTINESS

1  U. K. Le Guin, *The Wave in the Mind* (Boston, MA, 2004), p. 219.

2  P. Shaw, *The Sublime* (London, 2006), p. 3.

3  J.-F. Lyotard, 'The Sublime and the Avant-Garde', in *The Sublime*, ed. and trans. S. Morley (London, 2010), p. 37.

4  G. Dyer, 'The American Sublime', in *Working the Room* (London, 2010), p. 117. In the USA this book is titled *Otherwise Known as the Human Condition*.

5  R. Saner, *Reaching Keet Seel* (Salt Lake City, UT, 1998), p. 70.

6  S. Batchelor, *Verses from the Center* (New York, 2000), pp. 50–51.

7  Unfortunately Verdier's memoir of her apprenticeship is currently out of print in English translation. It is only available in French: *Passagère du Silence* (Paris, 2005).

8   F. Jullien, *The Great Image Has No Form; or, On the Nonobject through Painting* (Chicago, IL, 2009), p. 239.

9   G. Steiner, *Real Presences* (London, 1989), p. 95.

10  Ibid., p. 97.

11  Ibid., p. 202.

12  Ibid., p. 209.

13  R. Calasso, *Ka* (New York, 1998), p. 368.

14  This comes from a letter to Sigle Kennedy dated 14 June 1967, in S. Beckett, *Disjeta* (New York, 1984), and the quotations refer to two philosophers, the first to Democritus, the second to Arnold Geulincx.

15  S. Beckett, *Dream of Fair to Middling Women* (Dublin, 1992), p. 138. This was Beckett's first novel, which was not published for many years.

16  For this and for much else in the following paragraphs I am most grateful to Professor James Knowlson for generously sharing his personal tales of Beckett.

17  S. E. Contarski in the introduction to his edited *Samuel Beckett: The Complete Short Prose, 1929–1989* (New York, 1995), p. xxv.

18  Ibid., quoting from 'Text 4'.

19  Ibid., p. xxix.

20  S. Beckett, *Texts for Nothing* (London, 2010), p. 167.

21  D. Patterson, *Orpheus* (London, 2006), pp. 65–6.

22  Ibid., p. 69.

23  R. M. Rilke, from the '9th Duino Elegy', in *A Year with Rilke* (New York, 2009), trans J. Macy and A. Barrows, p. 216.

24  D. Patterson, 'The Dark Art of Poetry', T. S. Eliot Lecture 2004, at www.poetrylibrary.org.uk, accessed 18 September 2011.

25  M. Kundera, 'The Novel and Procreation (Gabriel García Márquez)', in *Encounters: Essays* (London, 2010).

26  V. Woolf, *Between the Acts* (London, 2005). The quotations from Jackie Kaye come from the introduction to this edition, pp. xi–xv; from the novel itself, 'scraps, orts', p. 117; 'try ten minutes', p. 111; 'let's break the rhythm', p. 115, 'Empty, empty', p. 22.

27   P. Mercier, *Perlmann's Silence* (London, 1995), p. 485.

28   Despite his own dislike for acknowledging citation, these quo-
     tations come from D. Shields, *Reality Hunger* (London, 2010),
     pp. 113, 31.

29   T. T. Williams, *Finding Beauty in a Broken World* (New York,
     2008).

30   M. Kwon, 'Rooms for Light, Light on its Own', in *James
     Turrell*, exh. cat., Gagosian Gallery, London (2011), p. 66.
     The term 'dematerialization' for such art movements has been
     well described by L. Lippard, *Six Years* (Berkeley, CA, 1973).

31   The Sartre quote comes from M. Restellini, *L'Essentiel.
     Giacometti et les Étrusques*, exh. cat., Pinacothèque de Paris
     (2011), my translations.

32   Adams, *Winter Music*, p. 74. J. L. Adams (Middletown, CT,
     2004).

33   Ibid., p. 113.

34   L. Joon, in *Void in Korean Art*, exh. cat. (Seoul, 2007), n.p.

35   Ibid., p. 166.

36   James Turrell, *Deer Shelter*, exh. cat., Yorkshire Sculpture Park
     (2006).

37   James Turrell press release, www.gagosian.com, October 2010.

38   This comes from an abridged version of a conversation
     recorded at the Museum of Contemporary Art San Diego
     on 27–28 March 2006, between Olafur Eliasson and Robert
     Irwin, reproduced in 'Take Your Time: A Conversation', in
     M. Grynsztejn, ed., *Take your Time: Olafur Eliasson*, exh. cat.,
     San Francisco Museum of Modern Art, San Francisco, and
     London (2007), p. 51.

39   A. Kiefer, lecture given on 10 January 2011 to mark his
     appointment by the Collège de France to the Chair of
     Creativity in Art (2010–2011), in *The Waves of Sea and Love*,
     trans. A. Coldhammer, exh. cat., White Cube, London (2011),
     p. 79.

40   Ibid., p. 82.

41   Ibid., p. 83.

42   Homi Bhabha, 'Making Emptiness', www.anishkapoor.com,
     accessed 12 August 2013.

43 From 'Out of Orbit', a report by Peter Aspden, *Financial Times Magazine*, 12/13 May 2012.

44 T. McEvilley, 'Seeds of the Future: The Art of Antony Gormley', from Antony Gormley, '*Field* and Other Figures, Modern Art Museum of Fort Worth, Texas, 1993', www.antonygormley.com.

45 Interview with Pierre Tillet, 2008, from Antony Gormley, 'Between You and Me', Kunstal Rotterdam, Netherlands, 2008, www.antonygormley.com.

46 Interview with Hans Ulrich Obrist, 2008, from Antony Gormley, 'Marco', Mexico, 2008, www.antonygormley.com.

47 S. Batchelor, 'Seeing the Light. Photography as Buddhist Practice', in *Buddha Mind in Contemporary Art*, ed. J. Baas and M. J. Jacob (Berkeley, CA, 2004), p. 141.

48 Quotations here come from the legends that accompanied the exhibits. *The Sonic Shadow* and *United States of Nothing* were still on show in October 2011.

49 R. Rugoff, 'How to Look at Invisble Art', in *Invisible: Art about the Unseen, 1957–2012*, exh. cat., Hayward Gallery, London (2012), p. 27.

50 Alex Ross, *And the Rest is Noise* (New York, 2007), p. 214.

51 J. Baas, *Smile of the Buddha: Eastern Philosophy and Western Art from Monet to Today* (Berkeley, CA, 2005), p. 169.

52 Gann, *No Such Thing as Silence: John Cage's '4'33"'* (New Haven, CT, 2010), p. 191.

53 In R. Kostelanetz, *John Cage* (New York, 1970), p. 90, and cited in Gann, *No Such Thing*, p. 80.

54 M. Epstein, 'Sip My Ocean: Emptiness as Inspiration', in *Buddha Mind*, ed. Baas and Jacob, p. 33.

55 From the notes to the exhibition 'Gerhard Richter: Panorama', at Tate Modern, London, 6 October 2011–8 January 2012.

56 These quotations come from the programme notes by James M. Keller for a concert conducted by Michael Tilson Thomas with the San Francisco Symphony on 23–6 February 2011. I am most grateful to Mr Keller for his permission to quote from these notes.

57 This comes from an interview of 1971 between Cage and

R. Kostelanetz regarding the influence of Marshall McLuhan on Cage's music, to be found at www.ccutler.com; that last term relates interestingly to Plunderphobia, John Oswald's early precursor to sampling.

58 Meredith Monk page on www.amazon.com, accessed 20 February 2011.

59 See www.akramkhancompany.net, accessed 18 February 2011.

60 Epstein, 'Sip My Ocean', p. 35.

61 J. Danvers, *Agents of Uncertainty* (Amsterdam, 2012).

62 C. Bollas, *The Shadow of the Object* (London, 1986), p. 31.

63 A. Ginsberg, in *Beneath a Single Moon: Buddhism in Contemporary American Poetry*, ed. K. Johnson and C. Paulenich (Boston, MA, 1991), p. 99.

64 R. Foster, 'Seamus Heaney Remembered', *The Observer*, 1 September 2013.

### EIGHT: EMPTY CONCLUSIONS

1 M. Boss, 'Martin Heidegger's Zollikon Seminars', *Review of Existential Psychology and Psychiatry*, XVI/1–3 (1978/9).

2 M. Boon, *On Copying* (Cambridge, MA, 2010), p. 247.

3 P. Hadot, *Philosophy as a Way of Life* (Oxford, 1995), p. 265.

4 T. Mettzinger, *The Ego Tunnel* (New York, 2009), p. 235.

5 Montaigne, Book 2, I. Translated by Stephen Batchelor (personal communication).

6 This comes from a letter to a friend, in R. Gittings, ed., *Selected Poems and Letters of John Keats* (London, 1966), pp. 40–41.

7 D. Loy, *Nonduality* (New Haven, CT, 1998), p. 174.

8 M. Abe and N. Waddell, ed. and trans, *The Heart of Dogen's Shobogenzo* (Albany, NY, 2002), p. 40.

9 T. Merton, *Dancing in the Water of Life* (San Francisco, CA, 1997), p. 223.

10 A. Einstein, 1921, as quoted by Professor R. Davidson in a talk given at Faces Conference San Diego, October 2010.

11 Santideva, *Guide to the Bodhisattva's Way of Life*, trans. S. Batchelor (Dharamasala, 1979), p. 118.

12  Marcus Aurelius, *Meditations*, 7.13, quoted by Hadot, *Philosophy as a Way of Life*, p. 198.

13  G. Vattimo, in R. Rorty and G. Vattimo, *The Future of Religion* (New York, 2005), p. 46.

14  Personal communication, quoting from his own *Living With the Devil*.

15  Ethics: Part II, Prop. XLIV.

16  J. Garfield, 'Study and Practice with Nagarjuna's Dharma', BCBS *Insight Journal*, 13 September 2011, www.dharma.org.

17  G. Steiner, *My Unwritten Books* (New York, 2008), p. 208.

18  M. Epstein, 'Sip my Daisy', in *Buddha Mind in Contemporary Art*, ed. M. Baas and M. J. Jacob (Berkeley, CA, 2004), p. 35.

19  A. Dillard, *Pilgrim at Tinker Creek* (New York, 1974, 1988), p. 258.

20  T. T. Williams, in *Writing Natural History*, ed. E. Leudars (Salt Lake City, UT, 1989), p. 50.

21  Batchelor, *Verses from the Center* (New York, 2000), p. 22.

22  Ibid., p. 21.

# BIBLIOGRAPHY

Abe, M., *Zen and Western Thought* (Honolulu, HI, 1985)
——, and N. Waddell, eds and trans, *The Heart of Dogen's Shobogenzo* (Albany, NY, 2002)
Adams, J. L., *Winter Music* (Middletown, CT, 2004)
Austin, J. H., *Selfless Insight* (Cambridge, MA, 2009)
Baas, J., *Smile of the Buddha* (Berkeley, CA, 2005)
——, and M. J. Jacob, eds, *Buddha Mind in Contemporary Art* (Berkeley, CA, 2004)
Barthes, R., *The Neutral*, trans R. E. Krauss and D. Hollier (New York, 2005)
Batchelor, S., trans., *Guide to the Bodhisattva's Way of Life* (Dharamasala, 1974)
——, *Buddhism Without Beliefs* (New York, 1997)
——, *Verses from the Center* (New York, 2000)
——, *Confessions of a Buddhist Atheist* (New York, 2010)
Beckett, S., *The Complete Short Prose, 1929–1989*, ed. S. E. Contarski (New York, 1995)
——, *Texts for Nothing* (London, 2010)
Blanchot, M., *The Infinite Conversation*, trans. S. Henson (Minneapolis, MN, 1993)
Bodhi, Bhikkhu, *The Collected Discourses of the Buddha* (Boston, MA, 2000)
Bollas, C., *The Shadow of the Object* (London, 1987)
Boon, M., *In Praise of Copying* (Cambridge, 2010)
Boonchang, Koo, *Portraits of Time* (Seoul, 2004)
Brenan, G., *St John of the Cross* (Cambridge, 1972)
Broks, P., *Into the Silent Land* (London, 2003)
Budick, S., and W. Iser, *Languages of the Unsayable* (Stanford, CA, 1987)

Calasso, R., *Ka: Stories of the Mind and Gods of India* (New York, 1998)

Callicott, J. Baird, and R. Ames, eds, *Nature in Asian Traditions of Thought* (Albany, NY, 1989)

Chuang Tsu, *Inner Chapters*, trans Gia-Fu Feng and J. English (London, 1973)

Conche, M., *Pyrrhon ou l'apparence* (Paris, 1994)

——, *Tao Te king* (Paris, 2003)

Coward, H., and T. Fosshay, eds, *Derrida and Negative Theology* (Albany, NY, 1992)

Danvers, J., *Agents of Uncertainty* (Amsterdam, 2012)

Davenport, G., trans., *Herakleitos and Diogenes* (San Francisco, CA, 1976)

Davidson, R., and S. Begley, *The Emotional Life of Your Brain* (New York, 2012)

Derrida, J., *Margins of Philosophy*, trans. Alan Bass (Chicago, IL, 1982)

Dillard, A., *Pilgrim at Tinker Creek* (London, 1976)

Dowman, K., trans., *The Flight of the Garuda* (Boston, MA, 1994)

Dreyfus, H., *Being-in-the-World* (Cambridge, MA, 1991)

Droit, R-P., *Astonish Yourself*, trans. S. Romer (New York, 2002)

Dyer, G., *Working the Room* (Edinburgh, 2010)

Epstein, M., *Thoughts Without a Thinker* (New York, 1995)

——, *Psychotherapy Without the Self* (New Haven, CT, 2007)

Fox, M. *Breakthrough: Meister Eckhart's Creation Spirituality in New Translation* (New York, 1980)

Gann, K., *No Such Thing as Silence* (New Haven, CT, 2010)

Garfield, J. L., *Empty Words* (Oxford, 2002)

Govinda, Lama, *Creative Meditation* (London, 1977)

Hadot, P., *Philosophy as a Way of Life*, trans. Arnold Davidson (Oxford, 1995)

Hanson, R., *Buddha's Brain* (Oakland, CA, 2009)

——, *Hardwiring Happiness* (New York, 2013)

Harding, S., *Animate Earth* (Totnes, Devon, 2006)

Heidegger, M., *What is Called Thinking?*, trans J. G. Gray and F. A Capuzzi (New York, 1968)

——, *On the Way to Language*, trans. P. D. Hertz (San Francisco, CA, 1971)

——, *Basic Writings*, ed. and trans. D. Krell (New York, 1972)

——, *Country Path Conversations*, trans. B. Davis (Bloomington, IN, 2010)

Heraclitus, *Fragments*, trans. T. M. Robinson (Toronto, 1987)

——, *Fragments: The Collected Wisdom of Heraclitus*, trans. B. Haxton (New York, 2001)

Humphries, J., *Reading Emptiness* (Albany, NY, 1999)

Huntingdon, C. W., *The Emptiness of Emptiness* (Honolulu, HI, 1983)

Johnson, M., *The Body in the Mind* (Chicago, IL, 1987)

——, *Moral Imagination* (Chicago, IL, 1993)

Johnson, K., and C. Paulenich, eds, *Beneath a Single Moon* (Boston, MA, 1991)

Jullien, F., *Vital Nourishment*, trans. A. Goldhammer (New York, 2007)

——, *In Praise of Blandness*, trans. P. M. Varsano (New York, 2008)

——, *The Great Image Has No Form; or, On the Nonobject through Painting*, trans. J. M. Todd (Chicago, IL, 2009)

Klein, A., *Meeting the Great Bliss Queen* (Boston, MA, 1995)

Kosko, B., *Fuzzy Thinking* (London, 1994)

Kundera, M., *Encounter* (London, 2009)

Kuzminski, A., *Pyrronhism: How the Ancient Greeks Reinvented Buddhism* (Lanham, MD, 2008)

Lakoff, G., and M. Johnson, *Metaphors We Live By* (Chicago, IL, 1980)

——, *Philosophy In the Flesh* (New York, 1999)

Larson, K., *Where the Hearts Beats* (New York, 2012)

Lawson, H., *Closure* (London, 2001)

Le Guin, U. K., *The Wave in the Mind* (Boston, MA, 2004)

Leuders, E., ed., *Writing Natural History: Dialogue with Authors* (Salt Lake City, UT, 1989)

Loori, J. D., *Hearing with the Eye* (Boston, MA, 2007)

——, *Making Love with Light* (Boston, MA, 2008)

Loy, D., *NonDuality* (New Haven, CT, 1988)

Lucretius, *The Nature of Things*, trans. A. E. Stalling (London, 2007)

McEvilley, T., *The Shape of Ancient Thought* (New York, 2002)

McGilchrist, I., *The Master and the Emissary* (New Haven, CT, 2009)
Macy, J., and A. Burrows, eds, *A Year with Rilke* (New York, 2009)
Magliola, R., *Derrida on the Mend* (West Lafayette, IN, 1984)
May, R., *Heidegger's Hidden Sources*, trans. G. Parkes (London, 1996)
Meillassoux, Q., *After Finitude*, trans. R. Brassier (London, 2008)
Mercier, P., *Night Train to Lisbon*, trans. B. Harshav (New York,
    2009)
——, *Perlmann's Silence*, trans. S. Whiteside (New York, 2012)
Merton, T., *Dancing in the Water of Life* (San Francisco, CA, 1997)
Metzinger, T., *The Ego Tunnel* (New York, 2009)
Montaigne, M. de, *Complete Works*, trans. D. M. Frame (London,
    2003)
Morley, S., *The Sublime* (London, 2010)
Mu Soeng, *The Heart of the Universe* (Somerville, MA, 2010)
Nanamoli, Bhikkhu, and Bhikkhu Bodhi, trans, *The Middle Length
    Discourses of the Buddha* (Boston, MA, 1995)
Nhat Hanh, T., *Heart of Understanding* (Berkeley, CA, 1988)
Nishitani, K., *Religion and Nothingness*, trans. J. van Bragt
    (Berkeley, CA, 1982)
Nussbaum, M., *The Therapy of Desire* (Princeton, NJ, 1994)
Olendski, A., *Unlimiting Wisdom* (Boston, MA, 2010)
O'Neal, D., ed., *Meister Eckhart, from whom God Hid Nothing*
    (Boston, MA, 1996)
Parkes, G., ed., *Heidegger and Asian Thought* (Honolulu,
    HI, 1987)
Patterson, D., *Orpheus* (London, 2006)
Robinson, M., *Absence of Mind* (New Haven, CT, 2010)
Rorty, R., and G. Vattimo, *The Future of Religion* (New York, 2005)
Ross, A., *And the Rest is Noise* (New York, 2007)
Russell, B., *The History of Western Philosophy*, 7th edn
    (London, 1971)
Saner R., *Reaching Keet Seel* (Salt Lake City, UT, 1998)
Sedley, A. A., and D. N. Long, *The Hellenistic Philosophers*
    (Cambridge, 1987)
Sells, M. A., *Mystical Languages of Unsaying* (Chicago, IL, 1994)
Shantideva, *Guide to the Bodhisattva's Way of Life*, trans.
    S. Batchelor (Dharamsala, 1979)

Shaw, P., *The Sublime* (London, 2006)

Silverman, H., ed., *Philosophy and Non-Philosophy since Merleau-Ponty* (London, 1988)

Snyder, G., *Poetics of Emptiness* in *House of K*, 9 (1989)

—, *Back on the Fire* (New York, 2007)

Stambaugh, J., *Thoughts on Heidegger* (Washington, DC, 1991)

Steiner, G., *Real Presences* (London, 1989)

—, *No Passion Spent* (London, 1996)

—, *Nostalgia for the Absolute* (Toronto, 2004)

—, *My Unwritten Books* (New York, 2008)

*Sutta-Nipata,* trans. H. Saddhatissa (London, 1985)

Thubron, C., *The Silk Road* (London, 2006)

Tucker, M. E., and D. R. Williams, eds, *Buddhism and Ecology* (Cambridge, MA, 1997)

Waley, A., *The Way and its Power* (London, 1934)

Wallace, B. Allan, *Buddhism and Science* (New York, 2003)

Watson, B., trans., *The Complete Works of Chuang Tzu* (New York, 1968)

Watson, G., *The Resonance of Emptiness* (London, 1998)

—, *Beyond Happiness* (London, 2008)

White, M., *Rites of Passage* (New York, 1978)

Woolf, V., *Between the Acts* (London, 2005)

Zajonc, A., ed., *The New Physics and Cosmology: Dialogues with the Dalai Lama* (Oxford, 2003)

# ACKNOWLEDGEMENTS

My profound thanks to, as ever and above all, Stephen Batchelor for inspiration and excellent suggested reading that took me off into the fascinating and shifting sands of Greek Scepticism; Sam Richards for his intimate knowledge of music historic and current; John Danvers, who has been exploring many of the fields covered here; Rick Hanson for encouragement and also precise reading and scientific knowledge, and wonderful discussions on the trail; Reb Anderson for a beautiful visit to Green Gulch and a memorable phrase about scientists seeking substance and finding emptiness; James Keller, for permission to quote from his excellent programme notes to a performance of Feldman's *Rothko Chapel*; and Wayne McGregor for great conversation regarding high-tech explorations into unknowing. Other friends have aided and encouraged me: Douglas and Tinker Mather; Kathy Phair, who shared a visit to the Museum of Modern Art in San Francisco seen through the eyes of emptiness; and Christine Collins, who introduced me to the living authority on Samuel Beckett, Professor Jim Knowlson, who entertained us with a wonderful afternoon of stories and manuscripts in Reading. Thanks too to Ben Hayes of Reaktion, a supportive and sensitive editor. Finally, my thanks to David, who was always there.